Anneila Menscher lives with her children on the east coast of Australia. Annelia has been a working single mother, an advocate, a mature-aged university student, and a leader in her career. Annelia believes strongly in empowering those around you. She does this by sharing her lived experiences with others through the written word.

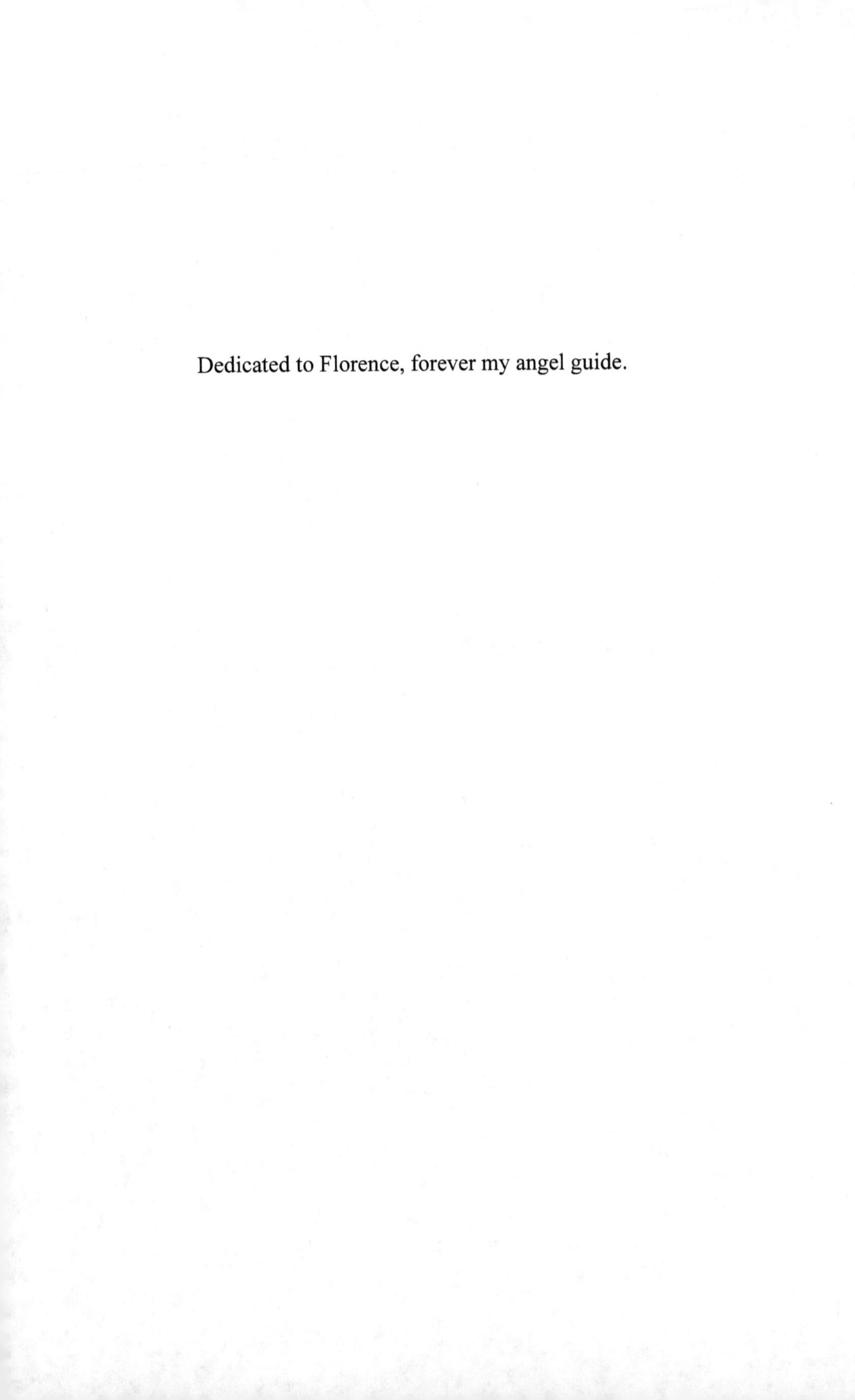

Dedicated to Florence, forever my angel guide.

Anneila Menscher

FORTY-FIVE

My Story

AUSTIN MACAULEY PUBLISHERS™

LONDON * CAMBRIDGE * NEW YORK * SHARJAH

A CIP catalogue record for this title is available from the British Library.

ISBN 9781035868339 (Paperback)
ISBN 9781035868346 (ePub e-book)

www.austinmacauley.com

First Published 2024
Austin Macauley Publishers Ltd®
1 Canada Square
Canary Wharf
London
E14 5AA

Table of Contents

Before you start reading, I want to state that all names in the following story have been changed. The story is true according to what I remember. Turns out, when you're looking back at your life so far, timelines can get fuzzy, and I seem to have been a bit busy in my 45 years.

All things I have learnt about myself in this story are based on me only. I am not a counsellor or therapist by any means. If you feel concerned about yourself, someone close to you or relationships that you are in, please seek professional help.

There is no shame in reaching out for help. Reaching out for help makes you stronger, it's the first step to getting your life back. It's the first step to becoming your own warrior.

Sometimes life just sucks, doesn't it? You think you have your future all mapped out and then BOOM! The universe says, 'Nope, that's not what's going to happen', and before you know it, your world gets completely upended and you're left standing there thinking what the fuck. Actually, to be more accurate, I would say that you feel like you are left standing on a small piece of land that's just big enough for your feet to fit on. You feel like that land is tethering atop a really tall and thin column of crumbling and rocky earth; you're wobbling over a bottomless abyss while torrential rain pours from the storm clouds that appear only directly above your head.

Tears cascade from your eyes, mascara runs in black rivers down your face, and you just can't help but think 'What the fuck has just happened?'.

That's happened to me several times in my life, and I'm sure it's happened to you too. It happens to all of us, just in varying degrees. Shit just happens. And while we are struggling to comprehend how life will become happy again, we do become happy again. We really have no idea how we are ever going to be able to breathe again, but we do breathe again. Somehow, we get ourselves off of that small patch of ground and get our feet onto solid ground so big, that we can see the earth blend with the horizon.

We get ourselves out from underneath the rainclouds, we get rid of the panda eyes, and we start walking under sunny skies with smiles on our faces. And usually, after we have felt like our world was crumbling around us when we pick ourselves up and move forward, we are a stronger version of ourselves and life gets better than we could have hoped for.

I know my story must be similar to most other women out there in some way or another. In some ways, I hope it's not, because parts of my story aren't really that good. But in other ways, I am fully aware that there are women out there, possibly like yourself, who have lived through worse situations in life. I respect you all, I acknowledge you all. In my story, I am not undermining anyone else's situation, I'm simply telling my story. This is my story as it was for me. It is my lessons, my tough times, my fun times. It's my growth, yet I am still growing.

I am blessed to live in Australia. I grew up with my parents being together and lived in a family home until I moved out to live on my own. I have one sister, who drives me absolutely nuts, but I love her; while sometimes I'm convinced that I love her out of sisterly obligation, I would move heaven and earth for her. I went to Sunday School and Youth Groups until I was about 15 years old. My best friend at that time was the minister's daughter who ended up having an affair with a married policeman before we got out of our teenager years. I only went to one primary school and one high school. I never moved house as a child. I was a straight-A student at school.

I was accepted into a 'special' school that had accelerated learning for gifted students. I refused to point blank to go to the special school and went to the local high school with all my friends instead. My teachers were trying to get me to study law or medicine and I'm sure I broke their hearts when I dropped out of school after Year 10 and worked as a checkout chick at a local community supermarket. I always had friends around me. I loved my family and visiting my grandparents during school holidays. They lived about five hours away which was hard. My nan was, is and always will be my hero.

My cousins all lived closer to our grandparent's place and would all visit nan and pops while my sister and I were there, and we loved it. School holidays were wonderful. It was a pretty normal childhood; it was a really good childhood. I have some incredible memories. I was very lucky.

And then, I grew up.

I'm going through a bit of a tough time at the moment. My partner and I have separated, he moved out. Before he left, things were completely shitty. The relationship wasn't working well at all, we both felt like we were using each other. For me, it was like he was using me to be the maid and look after his daughter. For him, it was like I was using him to help pay the bills.

After Luke left, I realised where we went wrong in our relationship—we didn't communicate with each other properly. He wouldn't make any effort with me and when things were hard, I stopped making that extra effort for him. When things got too 'real' and hard, we would both withdraw into our little protective shells and hide from confrontation. The proverbial shit would hit the fan and we would ignore each other for a couple of days, then one of us would start talking to the other, we would ignore what the problem was and we would just get on with life.

This happened many, many times, but the tension and stress just seemed to get worse every time. We never addressed our problems, we never resolved them or learnt how to grow from them. We avoided anything confrontational, which ironically led to the biggest arguments. After a couple of days of silent treatment, we would just throw a band-aid on our problems and move on and neither of us realised just what damage we were doing long-term.

Short-term we had avoided a difficult discussion that would have more than likely led to an argument. Long term, we were creating resentment and a gap that widened with every band-aid that we put on it.

This realisation has led me to think about past relationships, and how things have been before. Is this a trait of avoiding confrontational conversations and situations something that I have learnt over time, or have I had it all along?

I have been wondering if I am really such a bad person. I have questioned whether there is truth in all the nasty things I've been told about myself by the men in my life and all those other horrible, harmful things we think about ourselves. Was I too fat? Too loud? Too quiet? Not smart enough? Too smart? Not sexy enough? Did I try too hard? Did I not try hard enough? Did I bore him? Did I snore? Did I fart in my sleep all the time? Did my cooking suck? Was I not adventurous enough? Were my suggestions too adventurous? Was my hair the wrong colour? Was I too independent? Was I too needy?

Blah, blah, blah, I'm sure you can add some of these horrible, negative, soul-destroying questions and thoughts that we all ask ourselves. It's taken me a couple of days but I have slapped those thoughts out of my head (thanks to what has been probably too much alcohol) and I am just struggling to figure out what the hell is happening right now.

When Luke came over to get more of his things to take to his new place the other day, I put my big girl panties on, held onto my slightly shaking hands, and ignored the swamp of butterflies that were bouncing off every internal wall my body possesses and took a deep breath. I opened my mouth and spoke to him. And you know what? Starting those tough conversations was hard but continuing those conversations was easy. What the fuck was I worried about all those other times?

He has never made me feel threatened; I have never been scared by him or feared him, I just didn't speak up. And might I add, neither did he. Why hadn't I spoken up before? Why had I held back from talking? Was it because I didn't start these conversations the very first time the shit hit the fan that I was finding it harder and harder to start them? I don't know.

While he was gathering some of his things, I told him how I felt about the situation, what I have learnt about myself and also our relationship, and that I believe if we are honest with each other, if we allow ourselves to be vulnerable with each other and actually communicate, we can make it work and we would have a truly amazing relationship. After all, if things were good before and our only problem was not being able to sort our shit out, then that's something that we can work on quite easily, and our relationship could be spectacular.

He didn't say no to that but he didn't say yes either.

He has now been gone two weeks and we have had contact via texts, phone calls or seeing each other every day up to yesterday. I have scared him with my aggressive approach to fighting for us (he did admit this to me), so I put on another pair of big girl panties (who knew I had so many pairs?). I texted him to say that I was giving us space, I stopped communicating with him and have done my best to stalk him online ever since.

Heads up, readers, online stalking is the worst thing we can do, and you all know it. If the person we are stalking is online, we automatically think they're talking to someone; if they're not online, we think they're meeting someone. No matter what we see online, we always make it worse for ourselves. Yet when this stuff happens, what do we do? We stalk.

Why does he need to be on Facebook, on and off, constantly all day? Mind you, I am as well while I'm stalking him. Is he stalking me too? I am my own worst enemy at times. He and I love each other, and I do believe we can work through things and get back together, and if we do, we will have an incredible relationship built on strong foundations and we will never be in this horrible mind fucking place again. Space is vital right now.

While my heart is telling me to grab a boombox and go stand outside his house in the rain, hold the boombox over my head and stand next to my car "Say Anything" style while I wait for him to notice how incredible I am, the logical part of my mind is telling me if he can't see me active online if he doesn't hear from me or know what I'm doing, it will be nice for him for a day or two but after that, he will start wondering where I am, what I'm doing, who I am with; he will miss me. God, I hope the logic is right. I so badly want him to miss me,

I want him to call me, I want him to come back. We will have to wait and see. I have to be patient. And I'm learning that I'm not a very patient person.

To add to the mix, we are in a Covid lockdown, and I feel like I'm going insane. At the moment, I am grateful for the lockdown, all the pubs are shut which means Luke can't go out, drink and pick up some younger, more gorgeous, perfectly-toned supermodel so he can try to get me out of his system. I am thankful that I am working from home too, I don't have to explain the puffy red eyes to anyone at work.

So, while I'm waiting to find out if he will give us a chance to work on us and be the amazing couple that I know we can be, I can only think of four options of what I can do while I give us the space that we need. These four things are things that might stop me from breaking down into tears at random and unfortunate times throughout the day as I have done for the majority of the last two weeks. These four things are:

1. Take up the offer of the younger man I met years before I met Luke. Billy and I had a friends-with-benefits type of situation. He is several years younger than me and definitely knows what he is doing in the bedroom. We kept in touch as friends without the benefits over the years and he has offered to help keep my mind off my current situation. I know that once Billy's hands are on me, I wouldn't be able to think of anything else except the incredible sensations that would be pulsing through my body under his touch, but would that really be a wise thing for me to do while I'm so head fucked?

2. Curl up in the foetal position under my home office desk and cry until I just can't cry anymore, then sleep there until I start crying again. I wonder if I could get food and alcohol delivered to under my desk?

3. Do some writing therapy and write out an honest recount of my relationships. Maybe I'll find a pattern that shows why they didn't work. Maybe I will learn a thing or two about myself.

4. Get plenty of exercise, lose weight and get myself back into the great figure I had when I met Luke. Next time he sees me, I plan on being trim, taut and terrific. I have already done the 2am online shop and should have some new dresses, skirts, tops and shoes arriving in the next few days.

While option 1 is very tempting, I have decided the healthy option is for me to do options 3 and 4.

Stop yelling at me, ladies! I can already hear you all saying I should be in Billy's bed letting him convince me how sexy he finds me and showing me all the amazing tricks he can do with his tongue that he showed me he can many, many years ago, long before I ever met Luke. I bet Billy is more talented now than he was before. That would only make me feel better for several hours. Yes, I did say several hours. There was never a quick time with Billy. It really wouldn't do me any good for my mental health after he finished having his wild and wicked way with me. I would be feeling worse than I do now. No, that is not an option at all.

In order to help me sort out my messy head, I'm doing option 3, the writing therapy. I'm going to write about all of my relationships, the short ones, the long ones, the ones where I don't know if they were actually relationships or not, the good ones, the bad ones and the in-between ones. All of them. Hopefully, throughout my story, I can give you an odd update here and there about what's happening with Luke. While we are still in the very beginning of this book, I will let you know right now that I am hoping with my whole heart and soul that Luke and I work out our mess and have a happy-ever-after life together.

I'm trying to retain some power in this but the ball is now in his court. I said I wasn't going to contact him, now I just have to try to keep myself occupied while I wait and see what he does.

Writing my story will help prevent me from contacting him too soon. I really hope he contacts me first. What amount of space is too little? What amount of space is too much? Will he think I don't care if he doesn't hear from me? Will he think I'm obsessive and too pushy if he does hear from me? Do I risk losing him by not contacting him? Do I risk losing him by keeping up the contact with him? This is so hard! I hope he contacts me before I contact him. This sucks. I'm 45 years old, why am I in this place in relationships and love? When I was a teenager, I thought being 45 meant sitting at home every night with my husband, living in the perfect house and having teenage kids. I am far from it.

I'm pretty sure I'm overthinking this way too much. And I really miss his cuddles.

Ok, readers, enough of my current pity party. Go and open that bottle of wine, preferably a nice red, a cabernet sauvignon, make yourselves a nice platter of delectable cheese—camembert and vintage cheddar would be my choice—add some nice crackers and perhaps some prosciutto, throw on some quince paste, some salami, and add some grapes to convince yourself that if there is fruit on the cheese board, then it's healthy. Have a glass of wine, refill it and sit back to read. Trust me, the wine will make the story sound more interesting than it probably really is.

Join me as I take a stroll down relationship memory lane.

Chapter 1
George, My First Boyfriend

George and I met in high school. I was 15 and he was 16. High school sweethearts sounds so nice, doesn't it? Hmmm. I do know there are couples out there that were high school sweethearts and their lives seemed to be happy and they stayed together, and everything seemed just peachy; but spoiler alert, that wasn't the case with us. I guess it's not really a spoiler alert, it's too early in my story for everything to have worked out with George, especially when I've just told you how I'm pining like a lost puppy over Luke.

I still remember the day I first noticed George, or should I see the first day I became aware of George? I was on a roll call. Way back when I was in high school. Oh my god, it was 30 years ago! Back in high school, we began each day with a 15-minute class where students were grouped according to the first letter of their surname into classes of thirty kids to get their names marked off every day. Students in each roll call class ranged across all six years of high school from Year 7 to Year 12 in the same class group. I was in Year 9, I was fifteen years old and up to this point in my life, my love interests had mostly been big hair band rock musicians and surfer boys that appeared in the glossy teenage girly magazines.

On this particular day, I was leaving roll call class and one of the Year 11 guys came up to me and asked if my boyfriend was in the army.

"Huh?" was my reply. I didn't even know what the guy's name was, only that he was in Year 11 and his last name started with the same letter as mine. And what boyfriend was he referring to? And what made him think my non-existent boyfriend was in the army?

"Is your boyfriend in the army? Isn't that your boyfriend's army jacket you're wearing?"

At the second reference to my jacket, the penny dropped why he thought it was an army jacket. My dad was given some really cool jackets as part of his work uniform package. One of the jackets was the same green/khaki colour as my school uniform. When Dad had bought a new uniform package home, I had quickly claimed the jacket as my own and wore it to school to keep warm. Dad worked in industry, not in the army, and it never occurred to me that it resembled the army's khaki colour.

"Ah, no. I don't have a boyfriend," I'd replied and walked away without a second thought.

He caught up to me and grabbed my arm, stopping me. "That's good 'cause my friend likes you."

That stopped me in my tracks. Someone had noticed me and liked me? Daggy, nerdy, uncoordinated, unfashionable, braces-wearing me? Nah, this guy had to be playing a joke on me.

"It's true," he continued. "My mate likes you."

"How does your mate know me?"

"We hang out near the English classrooms during lunch and recess. He has seen you across the quad."

The English classrooms were in fact across the quad from where my friends and I hung out every break time. But still, why would someone notice me? I was the plain Jane girl in the group.

I was still calling bullshit, this couldn't be true. Surely they were having a bit of fun at my expense? I thought I'd try to call his bluff.

"Ok then," I told my fellow roll call classmate who's name I still didn't know. "If your mate likes me, you tell him to sit by himself on the silver seat where you guys hang out at lunch time today and I'll come over and say hi."

He nodded, smiled, and I walked away from him wondering why these guys were picking on me. Was I really that much of a dag? Was there some sort of contest I didn't know about where these guys were trying to see who could get the dorkiest girl?

I can't remember much about what happened between that moment after roll call class and lunch time, but I do remember what happened at lunch.

In the quad where we all had to hang out for our lunch and recess breaks, there were classrooms closing on three sides of the quad. At the fourth side of the quad was a walkway that led to the back entrance of the school. There were seats lining around the perimeter so everyone who was sitting down during the breaks was pretty much facing the centre of the quad.

Where George hung out with his big group of friends was the entrance into the English and History building at the bottom end of the quad. The group of Year 11 people had a covered walkway, a couple of silver seats and plenty of space to hang around and talk to each other. There were probably about fifteen to twenty people there hanging out, both boys and girls, during every break time we had throughout the day. I'd never really paid any attention to the people in that group, I'd just noticed 'the group' in passing.

Where I hung out with my group of ten or twelve friends was almost immediately across the quad outside a demountable classroom that had its own covered walkway, which joined up to the walkway that led into the building where George was.

This particular lunch break, I went into the demountable classroom and hid where I could see George but he couldn't see me. Sitting on the floor and peeking out of the window gave me a great vantage point to check out what happened during the lunch break.

As I sat in hiding for the entire lunch break, I watched as George sat on the silver seat by himself; you wouldn't believe it, he did this for the whole lunch break. George was about the same height as me, with light brown hair, and blue eyes; he wore a bright blue surfie hat and board shorts instead of the school uniform shorts. A few times people went over to talk to him and he shooed them away. He sat there the whole 40 minutes of the lunch break. Maybe he and his mate weren't teasing me? What was going on? Surely he couldn't actually like me, could he? What was I going to do? Was this for real? Why would he have wasted his whole lunch break?

The bell went signalling the end of lunch; we all grabbed our school bags and went off to our next class. I thought about it on and off but decided there was really nothing in yet; after all, why would he like a girl like me?

The next morning in roll call, George's mate came over to talk me again. "Why didn't you talk to George yesterday?" He asked.

"I thought you guys were just teasing me."

"Nah, he likes you and wants to talk to you."

Shit. Was this for real? Curiosity got the better of me and I agreed to talk to George.

I can't remember when the first time I actually spoke to George was. I can't even remember the first time he kissed me. I guess that speaks volumes for how our relationship ended up turning out. You'll find out about that a bit further into my story. What I do remember is when we got around to having our first kiss, it didn't quite go as I had seen kisses go in the movies. I didn't know what I should be doing, or how I should be doing it. Were we meant to be using tongue? Were our lips meant to be opened or closed? How much were we meant to open our mouths? What did I do with my hands? How was I going to breathe? How long should a kiss last?

I was so confused and I really didn't want to be doing it wrong. Our noses bumped, our lips briefly touched and just stayed joined, slightly open and not moving. It didn't seem like that's the way it should go. It looked so different in the movies.

I remember running up to my best friend's house as soon as I got home. She lived two houses away and I begged her to help me learn how to kiss. After we had grabbed each other's hands, jumped up and down and squealed in excitement that I had gotten my first kiss (as girls do), we ended up talking to her mum. I'll never forget this next part, and how her mum got through this without laughing I will never know.

I bow down to you, Mrs H, you got us through the lesson without making me feel like a complete and total nitwit, and you got through it without laughing at us. You are amazing.

My best friend and I went to talk to her mum and begged her to teach me how to kiss. Mrs H smiled at us and tried to assure us that if we just relaxed and let the guy control the kiss, everything would naturally happen and explained that we really shouldn't overthink it.

Our 15-year-old teenage brains couldn't comprehend that amazing piece of advice. It wasn't until after gaining more experience that I realised just how good the advice was. Mrs H ended up using the side of her wrist near the base of her thumb to show us some of her kissing techniques. It was weird watching my bestie's mother kiss her own wrist but it helped. The rest of that particular afternoon was spent with me practising kissing on my wrist while my friend watched and offered advice. Mouth closed, mouth open, tongue in, tongue out. I'm sure the area between my thumb and my wrist was feeling incredibly violated that day. But the mission was accomplished and I felt more confident that next time I was kissed, I would be able to do a better job at it.

Actually, hold that thought. The memory just flashed back to 12-year-old me. I was in Year 6, my last year at primary school. There was a big group of us that all hung around together. Boys and girls.

There was all this talk throughout the cool kids, which we definitely weren't, about how a boy would take a girl down behind the demountable building at the back of the playground and kiss her. The way everyone gossiped about it made it all sound so exciting but also so naughty at the same time. It was just outrageous for 12-year-olds to be doing this stuff, let alone talking about it. Girls would gossip and blush, boys would pretend to be cool while trying to figure out how they could get a girl to go behind the demountable with them for a quick pucker-up.

Kirk was a boy in our group. He was the same age as me and had sandy brown hair and brown eyes. He also had the neatest handwriting out of our entire class. The teacher used to make him walk around the whole room and show everyone just how neat his writing was. Isn't it strange what things you remember? I had some of the group over at my house one afternoon. Kirk's parents came to pick him up and I went to walk him out the front to say goodbye with a couple of the other girls that were leaving too. Kirk quickly turned around, kissed me on the lips (closed tight lips) with his hands in his pockets, and then he walked away.

Looking back on it, the kiss with 12-year-old Kirk was pretty much on par with the first kiss I'd experienced with 17-year-old George. Surely there had to be more to kissing than that?

A few days later as I walked by Kirk's desk to get to my desk in class, Kirk said hi then he told me I was dumped. That was the thing when we were 12 years old—a boy would ask you to go out with him, then for whatever reason he would turn around and say 'You're dumped'. Whenever a guy said this, his mates would laugh and the girls would be horrified. I swear boys used to ask you out so they could dump you, then get cheered on by their mates.

I just shrugged my shoulders and wasn't worried. I just kept walking to my desk and got on with what we were doing. I really had no idea what was going on anyway. Last I heard, Kirk had married and divorced one of the girls from our high school and he is now happily married to his husband.

Back to George.

I remember letting George walk me home from school. Turns out, he lived only a few blocks further down the road away from where I lived. In the morning, he would meet me at the corner near my house and we would walk to school together. We would smile at each other across the quad during lunch and recess and we would try to take detours in between classes so we could run into each other in the halls. We shared one classroom, it was our maths class with the same maths teacher. It turned out that we both sat at the same table in that classroom. How's that for a freaky Friday moment?

We used to write each other notes and leave them under the desk between the metal desk frame and the wooden desktop. His mate, the one who shared my roll call class, shared his maths class and sat in the next seat, and the tables were set up in formations of two desks and a row, all desks facing the front of the classroom. I was quite good at maths and was in the advanced mathematics class. Remember before I said I was a straight-A student? I am a bit of a nerd. You wouldn't believe it, the only time I ever studied for a test, I failed. I refused to study for an exam from then on and always got great grades.

I dread to think of what I could have achieved if I had really put my mind to it and tried. George wasn't that good at maths and was in one of the lower maths classes. He was two years ahead of me at school and the work I was doing was harder than what he was doing. Anyway, I have started to dribble, that really isn't relevant.

My parents didn't like me dating anyone, after all, I was only 15. George wasn't really the most parent-friendly person. He was shy and felt better by not coming to the house, he would usually wait outside the front gate for me or down by the corner. I wasn't really bothered by this, I was in Year 9 and I had a boyfriend that was in Year 11, I was over the moon! My parents were not impressed at all and tried to tell me how disrespectful his behaviour was. Since I was so love-struck, I couldn't see what they were trying to get me to see.

The year before meeting George, I had gotten a casual job at a local community supermarket in a neighbouring suburb. I was still working here after school and at the weekend when I was seeing George.

When I was working there on a Thursday afternoon after school, George would ride his bicycle up to stand outside the store and just look at me while I worked on the checkout. I felt pretty special. I was in such young puppy love. I was completely clueless with it all, really had no idea what was really happening, but I was loving it.

Now, for those of you who may be outside of Australia, the legal age for consensual sex in Australia is 16 years of age. The very day I turned 16 was the day he first tried his luck with me. I remember this very clearly. It was quite an educational morning.

Mum and Dad were both at work and my sister had already left to walk to school when George decided to come to the house instead of meeting me at the corner like usual. He wasn't going to school this particular day; I can't remember why but it was something that was happening in his family. Even though he wasn't going to school, he was still going to walk me there. I was ready for school when he got to my house but I didn't get to school on time.

George wished me a happy birthday and gave me a kiss and a cuddle. Writing this now, I only just realised that he didn't give me a birthday present! I went to grab my school bag and the next thing I knew, George and I were in my bedroom and we started kissing. We sat down on my bed and kept kissing. It was a good thing that we had found our rhythm with the kisses because we were doing a lot of it.

He laid me down on the bed and we kept kissing, though he didn't try anything else at first. He was laying on top of me. It was the first time ever I had a guy laying on top of me, and I remember telling him that his belt buckle was digging into my hip.

Now, this wasn't my finest moment in life. I honestly thought he was wearing a belt because there was this hard thing digging into my hip. He was wearing jeans, it was possible he was wearing a belt. It didn't occur to me that day that what was digging into me was actually his erection. That was the first time I had felt an erection against my body and I thought it was a belt buckle. Talk about being clueless! I shouldn't be too surprised though; at this time in life, I believed a blow job was when a guy used a hair dryer to dry the hair around his fun parts after a shower. To say I was a bit naïve is an understatement.

I made it clear to George that the clothes were going to stay on and nothing was going to happen, straightened up my clothing, wrote myself a late note, forged my mum's signature for the note and headed to school.

The roll call teacher questioned the signature on the note and asked me if it was really my mum's signature. "Yes, it is." I gulped with my fingers crossed behind my back.

"If I ring your mum and ask her if she signed this, would she say yes?" The teacher asked me.

Crossing my fingers even tighter behind my back, I nodded, "Yes, Ma'am."

The teacher looked at me intensely for a few seconds. She then nodded and warned me to be on time for the next day. Thank god for that. I'd gotten away with it. Phew.

Happy sweet sixteen to me. My day began with making out with my boyfriend and feeling an erection against my hip for the first time ever—even though at that time I still didn't know that it wasn't a belt buckle—forging my mum's signature for the first time (and only time I might add) and lying to my teacher. All these things were not like me at all.

A couple of months later, there was a school dance. The entire high school was invited to the dance in the school hall. My friends and I all went, and so did George and his friends.

The only effort in decoration for the occasion was the stands of disco lights appearing near the DJ on the stage. That was it. But with the hall lighting off, the music playing and everyone dancing, it was a lot of fun. George stated dancing close and kissed me. We stopped dancing and just kissed on the dancefloor. Almost straight away a teacher tapped us on the shoulder and we were taken to the principle's office for inappropriate behaviour. Nothing was said to George but I was given a lecture about what I was doing and the principle threatened to call my dad to see how my father felt about my behaviour.

I remember standing across the desk from the old fuddy-duddy of a principle, legs slightly apart, arms behind my back standing 'at ease'. On the outside, I was confident and unflinching as I told the principle that my dad would be ok with the phone call and I assured the principle that my parents knew about George and me and that they approved.

The principle asked for my parents' phone number and inside my entire body was trembling as I told him. Then I added, "They get up early for work, so you might need to let the phone ring for a while before they answer." My entire body sighed with relief as the principle hung up the phone without dialling the number. I was warned to make sure I exhibited appropriate behaviour in the future and was led back into the hall. Why didn't George get spoken to? Why didn't the principle threaten to call his parents?

Those questions disappeared from my mind when my bestie came up to me and told me that when George and I were kissing, it looked funny. She said it looked like he was trying to eat my face and I was trying to pull away. Oh no! I needed to get back to the drawing board with kissing. Perhaps more practice would be fun.

Chapter 2
Riley, My First Date

George and I were on-again off-again throughout the next year or so of high school. In between being each other's boyfriend and girlfriend, we would see other people. The alarm bells should have started going off about the relationship with George then, but they didn't. I really had no idea as to how badly I was being treated. I was just happy to have a boyfriend and to be honest, I liked the attention too. What I really should have done was I should have stopped looking at him with rose-tinted glasses and started to listen to those alarm bells that had begun ringing in my head.

Just to let you know, it wasn't a matter of breaking up with George one day and going out with someone else the next. While it might seem like I hopped straight from one guy to the next, I didn't. Riley happened about a month after a breakup with George.

One of the guys I dated was someone I worked with. He was a trainee manager at the supermarket where I worked. Riley was about a head taller than me, he had a big cheeky grin, sparkly brown eyes and sandy brown hair that curled where it sat on the collar of his work shirt.

He always seemed to be smiling and he always seemed to be in eye shot of the checkout that I worked on. He would chat with me whenever he got the chance. Me being me, I had no idea that he liked me in more than a work-friend kind of way. When he asked me what I did for fun at the weekend, I told him about roller skating.

My friends and I used to hang out at the local skatel every weekend. Every Friday and Saturday night, we'd be there skating around in circles, hanging out with all of our skating friends, and just having a good old time really. We were the 'regulars'. We knew everyone there and everyone knew us. We knew the staff by name, we felt like we ran the place. It was so much fun.

Riley joined us there one night. A couple of my friends and I fitted him and his mate up with some hire skates and we had a great night. Riley skated in laps around the rink. He'd wave or smile at me as he skated past while I was standing on the side of the rink, we would skate around together. I showed off a bit, and he showed off a bit, but there was no hand-holding or slow skating together. Being the naïve and clueless 16-year-old that I was, had no clue that Riley was doing this because he liked me and was trying to impress me. He had come along skating so he could spend some time with me outside of work and was trying to give me hints that he liked me, but I had no clue.

Poor Riley. He had no idea how oblivious I was. Because of my total lack of awareness about the whole boy likes girl thing, Riley thought he was friend-zoned, but to his credit, he didn't give up.

Eventually, after many, many hints from Riley and many elbow nudges from my friends, I realised that he truly wanted to take me out on a real date and not just a friend date. I could feel the blush rising in my cheeks as I said yes.

Riley was my first actual date. While I had been George's girlfriend for a while before this, George and I had never been on a real date together; we'd just hung out at school, at each other's houses after school and apart from when we would make out, we just went and did things with our group of mutual friends.

I can't remember what I wore on my first date with Riley, but it was the 90s, so I'm pretty sure it was a very cringe-worthy outfit and I am certain I had a perm left over from the 80s as well. Sounds pretty horrific, hey? Riley picked me up in his car. I was so excited that he had his licence and a car, it made me feel really grown up.

At this age, I was obsessed with reading teenage romance novels, most of which were written about American teenagers in high school, and on my first date, I felt like I was a character in one of these books.

Riley came to the front door of my parents' house and knocked. He met my parents, shook my father's hand, and we left.

My parents already liked him more than they liked George simply because Riley showed some respect to both them and myself by coming to the front door.

George used to just hang around the front gate until I would walk out. Riley came to the front door. Honestly, I should have realised the difference in respect between the two guys right then and there but I didn't.

Now, at the time, I had no idea really what to expect on a first date or even what Riley really thought about me. And I never really knew what he'd thought until we caught up many, many, many years later.

For my first date, Riley took me to Sizzler for dinner. For those who don't know, Sizzler was a chain of all-you-can-eat restaurants that gave everyone a slice of the most amazing cheese toast as they were seated. After dinner, at which I can still vaguely remember he had been incredibly sweet and gentlemanly, he took me to the movies to see *Point Break*, a hot new release movie starring Patrick Swayze and Keanu Reeves. I was sitting on his left side; he had chosen seats in the back row and off to the side for us to sit in.

I looked at him and smiled, he pretended to yawn, stretched his left arm high up in the air and bought it down around my shoulders, just like the boys did in the books I read. He never kissed me at the movies, in fact, he has never kissed me at all. But just the feel of his arm around my shoulders was enough for me to lose all concentration and I have no idea what happened in the movie after the point of the yawn, stretch and cuddle move. When the movie finished, we went to TimeZone to play some games and he got me home right on curfew.

At home, he got out of the car and opened my door, then we walked around the back of my parents' house and up the steps to the back door. He seemed nervous which made me begin to feel nervous. I thanked him for a great night, he did the same, then he smiled, turned around and walked away.

If I had gotten a goodnight kiss, I think it's safe to say that my first real date as a 16-year-old would have been pretty much perfect. Even though there was no good night kiss, it was still a pretty great first date.

George must have heard about my date with Riley as not long after this amazing first date George started talking to me again. I hadn't heard anything from Riley and didn't see him at work, so I assumed as there had been no good night kiss and no contact since that Riley wasn't interested in having a second date.

After a very short period of time where George was chasing me—and by very short I mean about five minutes—George and I were back on as boyfriend and girlfriend.

Now these days before mobile phones, there was no social media, no direct messaging, no Instagram or Facebook or Snapchat to keep in touch. There wasn't even any email. To contact people, we rang the home landline phone, wrote a letter or had to go to see them in person.

I didn't know that the reason I hadn't seen Riley at work was that he had been sent to another branch of our supermarket a few suburbs away that was short-staffed. When he got back to our store a few weeks later, he was told that I was back with George. He never put the pressure on for a second date. Got to give Riley credit though, we stayed friends until we both quit working at the supermarket. And we are still friends today, almost 30 years later.

About 10 years ago, Riley found me on Facebook and we have been in touch, we chat a bit here and there. He is married now and has two great kids with his gorgeous wife. He joined the army for a while after he left the supermarket and he now lives on interstate. I took my boys for a holiday about 8 years ago to a holiday destination near where Riley lived. Riley and I caught up for lunch with the kids and it was nice. There are some people who are in our lives forever, and I'm honoured to have Riley as a lifelong friend.

When we started talking again, Riley told me all about how he used to try to get to work with me when we were at the supermarket, especially when I was putting the stock on shelves and how he liked it when I had to climb up the stock ladders. It wasn't in a really gross pervy kind of way, I wore shorts or long pants to work so there was definitely no skirt to look up, it was in a sweet kind of way. He told me that he used to like me climbing the ladder so he got a good view of my butt and legs. Apparently, I had an amazing ass and legs when I was younger. Who knew? If I had been more aware of this and more confident about myself, then perhaps my love life may have been quite different.

He also told me about how he felt on the first date. I think it's very safe to say that his idea of the end of the night and my idea were very similar but very different at the same time. When laughed as he told me how he had been very nervous to ask me out and that he had been excited that I'd said I would go out with him. He wanted our date to be perfect and he had put a lot of planning into it. He was so sweet. He also told me that when he walked me to my parent's back door, all he could think about was giving me a good night kiss but he wasn't sure if I wanted him to kiss me or not. Riley said he had gotten scared, so he had just turned around to leave, and he had regretted not giving me that good night kiss.

As you've just read, I'd had no contact with Riley for a while after our date and then George and I got back together. This time with George didn't last too long. It seems George didn't really want me but he couldn't handle anyone else having me either. We broke up again. I don't remember why, but one thing I do remember is that I was never really heartbroken whenever we broke up. Similar to how I was with Kirk when I was 12, and Kirk had told me I was dumped; I just shrugged my shoulders and kept on going, not really sure what it was that was happening, not being too bothered. That was another alarm bell that I ignored. Insert massive forehead slap here.

Luke Update! He just sent me a message and asked if I was ok to chat. My stomach instantly plummeted all the way to the centre of the earth. My hands are shaking. Oh my god. This is it. He is going to tell me that he is done, he has found someone else. He is going to completely finish things over a phone call. How am I going to get through this? Its 7pm at night, is it too late to go buy a bottle of wine and drink myself into oblivion? He wants to chat? Was this a good thing? Was this a bad thing? I was instantly nervous and scared at the same time. Why was he asking if I was ok to chat? Why didn't he just call? He was giving me a warning, it must be a bad chat that he wants to have.

I replied to his text with a simple 'Ok'. As I hit send, I actually gulped. This is it. I grabbed some tissues, got comfy on the lounge, tried my best to stop my hands from shaking and stared at my phone waiting for it to ring. I don't think I even blinked, I just stared at it until it rang.

Facetime? Luke was Facetiming me? Did he want to see my face as he destroyed my heart?

I swiped right to answer the call. "How's it going?" He asked.

I looked at his face on the screen; god I missed him. I ached to wrap my arms around him and hold him close. He looked tired but he didn't look like he was just about to rip the remains of my heart from my chest and squish them up into a million shredded pieces.

"It's ok, how 'bout you?" I asked.

"Tired. How was your day?"

What the hell? He's asking about my day. I must have looked confused because he just looked at me for a few seconds and then he smiled at me. When he smiled, I realised he wasn't calling to break my heart, he just wanted to talk. We had only had no contact for two days and he was Facetiming me. Could he miss me? He still loves me! This was good, wasn't it? Suddenly, I was happy, I smiled at him and settled in for a good chat. The conversation was light-hearted and very generic, there was no discussion about what was happening between us at the moment.

Dear readers, I'm sure you as shaking your heads at my reaction, as I am now as I write about it. We've all been there but it's quite confronting to read in words what we do, isn't it?

Chapter 3
Eddie, My Introduction to Romance

How's that glass of wine going, readers? If I write this the right way, you should all be smiling at my Eddie chapter.

It was around the time of this last break up with George that my parents sat my sister and me down for a family chat. Turns out, my sister and I had a choice to make—did we want an inground pool put into the backyard or do we want to go on a family holiday to Bali? Ah, hello! That's a no-brainer. Bali, please!

The tickets were booked and a few months later, we flew across the country to board an international cruise ship, whose name I just can't pronounce so I won't write it in case I spell it wrong, and cruise our way to Bali.

Apart from a holiday to Queensland to visit mum's friends when I was a lot younger, this was our first big holiday, and I was so excited.

Now I can't tell you anything at all about our flight to the other side of Australia, I can't tell you how we got to the cruise ship terminal, and I can't tell you a thing about boarding the ship. But I can tell you that after the first night, the cruise was an amazing experience. The first night itself was spent with people holding their tummies and small brown vomit bags all magically appearing along all the handrails that lined every corridor on every deck of the cruise ship. It took me that first day and night to get my sea legs but by the second day, I had adjusted to the gentle sway of the ocean rocking the boat and I was ready to have a great time.

Not long into the cruise, I met some other people in their mid to late teen years. We all seemed to gravitate together with some sort of weird magnetic force. I don't know how we found each other but we did. There was a group of about eight of us and we ran amok across the cruise ship. Now I don't know if my parents had that much faith in me that they believed I would never do anything wrong or if they chose the whole ignorance is bliss approach to what I was doing, but they never argued when I took off to hang out with my new friends and they never asked what we were doing.

Maybe my parents just assumed that I was restricted to the boundaries of the cruise ship so I wouldn't get into mischief. Who knows? I was just grateful that I was allowed to spend the days with my new friends. And I had a great time. We weren't getting up to no good, not really. We were just exploring what the cruise ship had to offer us, enjoying ourselves, and just being a group of teenagers. Perhaps we found ourselves in some places we weren't allowed to be in, maybe we pushed some doors open without reading the door plaque that said 'Staff Only', but we didn't get caught. So did we really do it?

Eddie was one of the guys in our group. He was about 6 months younger than me, he played football and had a really nice athletic build. Being 16 ½ years old now, I had upgraded my teenage romance novel reading to regularly include more glossy teenage girl magazines and had developed quite a healthy appreciation of a nice, fit, tanned male body. Especially the surfer types that the magazines featured. Eddie had the sunkissed sandy brown-blonde streaked hair that was shiny and oh-so-soft to touch. His eyes were pools of chocolate brown and his smile lit up his whole face.

He looked just like the beach surfie-type male models that were featured in the teenage girl magazines that I bought every month. These magazines provided me with the sexy male model posters that I stuck to my bedroom walls alongside the music artist posters. Eddie's deep voice was very sexy to listen to and I have to say his lips were just perfect to kiss. We were instantly attracted to each other and became inseparable on that holiday.

Ah, the holiday romance.

There were a few hours through the day that we both spent with our own families and then while the parents would all sit back on deck chairs and enjoy the sunshine and endless ocean views with a good book and a drink, the group of us would meet up somewhere to enjoy our day. We'd meet the families again for dinner and then we'd be off again doing our own thing together until curfew time. Yes, even though we were on a cruise ship, we still had a curfew, though I think it was more enforced by the captain than it was enforced by our parents.

There was a movie cinema on one of the lower decks. One day, the whole group of new friends decided to go and check it out. We were the only people in the entire cinema and we sat in the back row to watch *Lawn Mower Man*. Not my ideal movie but I didn't complain as Eddie was sitting next to me holding my hand. His hand seemed to swallow mine in its warmth. My hand felt so small in his, it was wonderful. I was definitely the smitten kitten and couldn't stop smiling. He was just gorgeous.

Another time, we grabbed a table in the activities room and played bingo. Eddie and I were just getting on perfectly. I jokingly told him he had bingo and he jumped up onto the table, bingo card in his hand, and yelled bingo at the top of his lungs. He didn't have bingo but he had a great laugh about it. The fact that he laughed along with the joke just made my heart flutter that much more with him. Another time in that activities room, they had a disco going with a DJ playing music, the lights were dimmed and disco balls and lights appeared out of nowhere.

Eddie and I went there with the group and we were all dancing together in a big circle on the dancefloor. We were having a great time laughing and dancing, showing off moves and mimicking each other. We didn't have a care in the world.

Then the new Boys II Men hit, *End of the Road* came on. Some of the others left the dancefloor to sit down but Eddie pulled me in close. He wrapped his arms around me, I looped my arms over his shoulders. We were standing so close, that there wasn't a gap between our bodies at all. And he smelt really good.

To this day, I still think about that dance whenever I hear that song and I always smile. It was my first real slow dance. It was a slow dance that had full bodies touching, arms around each other, my head on his chest, his head nestled next to mine, bodies swaying slowly to the music with content smiles on our faces. It wasn't until writing that just now that I realised just how amazing that slow dance really was. Insert massive reminiscent sigh here. Great song, a great location, great guy. It was the perfect first slow dance.

Eddie and I spent as much time as possible together. We hid from the others so we could make out in any dark and quiet spaces we could find, and we hung out with the group doing whatever activities the cruise ship had to offer, and we had an absolutely amazing time.

And the kisses, have I mentioned the kisses yet? Eddie was the most incredible kisser. When our lips met, nothing else existed. He did incredible things to me when he kissed me.

When the cruise ship docked off the coast of Bali, we all went off with our own families to do our own explorations. There were smaller boats, like a shuttle service, that took us the rest of the way to Bali and we all went off exploring temples, monkey forests, markets and other Balinese delights. The shuttle boats took us back to the cruise ship at the end of the day and after dinner, we were able to all meet up again and hang out together until we had to go back to our cabins.

When the cruise ship left Bali and began cruising the seas back towards the Great Land of Oz, the group of new friends were all able to spend the majority of our days together again, which meant I was able to spend more time with Eddie.

The last night of the cruise was a night that none of us wanted to end, especially Eddie and I. When we woke up the next morning, we would be getting ready to go back to our homes. Would we ever see each other again after tonight?

As it was the last night on the ship, there was no curfew for any of us.

Eddie and I snuck off to have time to ourselves. There was a lot of kissing, a lot of promises to stay in touch and some tears from both of us. We decided we weren't going to go to sleep, we wanted to spend every remaining moment together. There would be plenty of time to sleep when we had to say goodbye the next day. It was the first time I ever stayed up all night and it was the first time I watched a sunrise with a guy. We sat outside on the same deck chair and held hands as we snuggled and held each other, the ocean breeze playing with our hair, our eyes wide open but tired, and yet not sleepy at all.

We watched the magnificent colours of sunrise change across the never-ending horizon while the water lapped at the cruise ship. We sat in silence, our silence saying so much, voicing our hope that our adventure together would never end, yet knowing we would both be going to sleep later that night in different states, a full day's drive apart. Those sunrise kisses were so tender and beautiful. They were slow and deep, full of promises and telling each other what our words just could not say.

For a 16-year-old, Eddie did the romance thing so very well. Almost perfectly in fact. Better than almost every other guy I have ever known, and that is to this day, not just when I was 16. Now as I'm writing this and remembering, I'm wondering if Eddie ruined me romance-wise for all other men. A 16-year-old me experienced the most amazing romance on that cruise with Eddie. The hand-holding, the most tender kisses, the laying back in his arms to watch the ocean, the dancing, the fun; did I mention the kisses? So many beautiful kisses. It's sad to say that no one has ever come close to the level of romance that Eddie did.

Perhaps it was being on the cruise, perhaps it seemed more romantic because we lived in different states and didn't know how we would see each other after the cruise ended. Maybe it was because we both knew there was an end date for us. Maybe it was because Eddie was just a pure romantic and had opened my eyes and my heart to the fact that romance wasn't just words in a book or a scene in a movie. Romance could be real, and it was incredible. Whatever the reason was, the romance level had hit maximum, and I totally loved it.

The flight home was horrible, all I wanted to do was cry. Being back at home was just as bad. Now remember back then, there were no mobile phones, no social media apps, and the only way to stay in touch was a letter, a phone call or a visit. Phone calls were expensive though. Eddie and I would take turns calling each other and we had to wait for when the long-distance phone calls went off-peak and were cheaper, which was usually after about 6pm at night and all day on a Sunday.

We could only talk on the phone once or twice a week and we had limited time to talk and we were in different time zones, his time zone was one hour behind my time zone at that time of year. Those days there was only one phone in the house and there was no call waiting; if someone else tried to call while you were on the phone, the caller would get the engaged signal and you wouldn't have any idea someone was trying to ring.

Our parents weren't too impressed with us staying on the phone for long periods of time. After about twenty minutes of talking and saying how much we missed each other, our parents would start to tell us to get off the phone. We would write letters to each other. I would get at least one letter from him every week. I loved getting home to find a letter with my name on it. I'd go straight into my bedroom, shut the door, and curl up on my bed to read his letter, then read it over and over again until I knew every word by heart.

Thinking back on this romance, I remember Eddie would send me packages through the post and in them he had gifts for me, but the thing I remember most from one of the packages was his jacket. He'd sent me his football jacket. It was red, and had some white markings on it; it smelt like him and I was so proud. He'd sent me his jacket. I'd felt like a cheerleader in an American high school movie when the guy gave the girl his jacket and that meant they were going steady. I couldn't stop smiling. In my romantic teenage mind, this meant I was his girl.

We kept up letters and phone calls and soon it was going to be my birthday. Now I can't remember how we approached our parents about the visit idea, or how we even managed to get them to say yes to it, but for my 17th birthday, Eddie flew to visit me on his own, and stayed with us, in his own room, of course.

The night before my birthday party, I took Eddie skating. He chatted with my friends; he fumbled on his skates but didn't give up, he fitted in well. All the girls were gushing over just how gorgeous he was, and I just couldn't stop smiling. When it was time for the slow skate, he grabbed my hand and I had my first couples skate to Guns N Roses song, *November Rain*.

For my birthday, my friends all joked that it was a fairy bread and red cordial party as my mum refused to let us have alcohol; even the kids in the group who were already over 18 and legally allowed to drink weren't allowed to drink at my party. To go along with the joke, we made up jugs of red cordial and plates of fairy bread and wouldn't you know it? Everyone loved it and we ran out of fairy bread.

After everyone had gone home from the party and Mum, Dad and my sister had gone to bed, Eddie and I headed to the lounge room to watch a movie together. Before too long, he was lying on the floor and I was half lying on top of him and we were kissing. God, he knew how to kiss. We kissed and kissed and kissed. We kissed some more. We made up for lost time with all those kisses. Slow and tender, teasing, tasting, whole-mouth kisses. There was never any worry about me not knowing what to do like when George first kissed me. Kissing Eddie was so easy and so magical. Oh, those slow kisses were incredible.

After a while, he began to play with my boobies and I liked it. I didn't really care that my parents were asleep in their bedroom and only a couple of rooms away from us. I let him play with my boobies and we just kept on kissing.

He grabbed my hand and slowly guided it down towards his tally whacker, and oh my god! It was so big! And so hard! And it felt hot! I pulled my hand away but I was curious. As he kept kissing me and torturing my nipples with his amazing touch, I slid my hand up under his shirt and was thrilled to touch the small sprinkling of hair on his chest. I slid my hand down his belly and kept going further down under his pants until I could feel the heat of his hard erection under my fingers again. He was so smooth and silky and so warm. It was my first time touching a tallywhacker without the barrier of clothing, I really didn't know what to expect. He was so hard, so silky and so warm to touch, and my curiosity grew, as did he (wink-wink, nudge-nudge).

You know how when you touch something like a nice fabric or something textured, like velvet or sand at the beach, and you enjoy the feel of it, so you keep stroking your fingers over it and you try different ways of running your fingers over it and around it to enjoy the feel of it under your touch? That's what I was doing with his tally whacker. He was just so nice to touch. Soon I was enjoying the feel of him with my whole hand and he didn't try to stop me, so I guessed he mustn't have minded me doing it. I hadn't done this before but my fingers seemed to instinctively know what to do.

I was stroking him slow, fast, hard, soft, tracing my fingers over him, grasping him with my whole hand. My fingers learnt his length and width, they trailed around the head and over the tip before closing around him in a whole hand grip. He was so nice to touch. Now, dear readers, I know you know what I was actually doing at this time, but remember back then, I was completely clueless and I had no clue what I was actually doing.

Our kisses became more intense, our breathing became quicker, heavier; it was feeling so, so good. My hand and fingers kept doing their own thing— moving, touching, sliding, grasping. Was it possible that he was getting harder? Both his hands were on my breasts, my nipples tight and firm under his touch.

Then Eddie held me tighter, his body seemed to tense, he made a weird noise and he stopped kissing me for a little bit, his lips open over mine, his breath hot and fast, his hands still on my breasts. As I moved my fingers back up his big silky tally whacker, I could feel this sticky gooey warm stuff spilling out around the top of his penis.

What had happened? Was he ok? What had I done? Had I broken it? Did he pee himself? What the hell had just happened?

He opened his eyes and looked at me, pure contentment in his smile. Hmmm…I thought about the situation, about what I knew about sex and the penis, and I wasn't too sure but I think I had just given my first-hand job. I figured he'd cum, and that's what the gooey sticky stuff was. If a hand job is what I had done, it must have been ok because he definitely wasn't complaining.

We kissed some more, I couldn't get enough of those kisses. The movie had long finished, and eventually, we went to our separate rooms to try and get some sleep.

Dad and I took Eddie back to the airport the next day and after a very teary goodbye, I never saw him again. The phone calls and letters slowly stopped over time. I don't remember if one of us ended it or if our romance just phased out.

Perhaps he met someone else? I wish I could remember what had happened that made our contact stop. Thinking back on this now, I am very, very impressed with the romance level he had. I'm pretty sure Eddie would have made someone a very happy woman. I hope he never gave up on being a romantic. And I'm even more sure that my love of everything romance, and my need to be romanced, began on a cruise ship while I was in Eddie's arms.

Eddie was my first slow dance, my first all-night date, my first sunrise, my first jacket, my first incredible kiss…he was my perfect introduction to romance.

Chapter 4
Tom and Steve, My
'I Don't Know What's'

Ok, dear reader, if you haven't put the book down yet, it might be time to top up your wine glass. This chapter is only going to be a short one.

Now before you start thinking I'm a bit of a tart, I will let you know that these guys were at different times and only for a very short period of time, and they were several months after the romance with Eddie had dwindled away to nothing.

These are two guys who I wasn't in a relationship with but they were both parts of the group I hung out with at skating and they both kissed me. Once each. One kiss only for these guys, and soon you will know why. I'm pretty sure as you read, you'll agree that one kiss was more than enough.

In the Riley chapter, I mentioned to you that my friends and I used to love roller skating and hung out at the skatel. There were different groups of regulars that had their own areas around the rink that they usually sat in. There was seating around the two long sides of the rink, a grandstand at one short end and a roller door at the other short end. My group had grown and there was quite a number of us as some of the other 'regulars' had merged into our group. After all, our group of 'regulars' was the coolest group there, or so we liked to believe. We generally took up most of one whole length of one of the long sides of the rink.

Our group ran that place. Pete, the owner, would get us to help out at the kiosk when they were busy. I used to love skating around behind the counter, serving other skater's hot dogs and cokes. The DJ would talk to us over the speaker system from his perch up high in his DJ box, calling us out by name as he watched us all skating around the rink below where he sat. We would yell out song requests, he'd play them providing they were Guns 'n' Roses songs. Those skating days were great times. We had no idea how good it was. Or how fit it kept us. I had the best figure of my life throughout those skating days.

One of the older guys in the group (and by older guys I mean the 18-year-olds) bought a friend along to the rink one night. Tom was tall, super skinny, had really short, almost crew cut short, blonde hair with a long curl in the front of his forehead, nice blue eyes, and a big nose. Weird how I remember the nose. He asked me if I wanted to skate and I said sure. Again, I really didn't think anything of it, I just figured it was a friend of a friend and that he and I would be friends. No other thoughts really popped into my mind.

Now, I should tell you that at this point, I was still completely oblivious to attention from guys. I just assumed all guys wanted to just be friends. I thought I was just daggy, a bit loud, average-looking, and overall just quite plain. But I did love to smile and laugh and just have fun. I had no clue what so ever that by just being me and smiling and having fun guys were noticing me and were finding me attractive.

I was 17 years old and was told by those magazines that I loved to read and those movies that I loved to watch that I needed to be skinny, gorgeous, fashionable, and wear makeup and all that stuff in order to be attractive to guys. I only wore mascara, I was daggy, I wasn't skinny, but I wasn't big either. My hairstyle was as simple, as my taste in clothes, and I wasn't fashionable by any means. I felt that I was average in every possible way. But I did like to smile, and to laugh and to have fun.

Now back to Tom. Tom was very gorky but also seemed sweet. We skated and had fun. Over a few weeks, he and I would talk and laugh and just enjoyed skating. I was having some skating friends over at my place one weekend and Tom came along too. As he left my house that night, he gave me a kiss on the lips. His lips were soft, they were closed. It was a slow and deliberate kiss and I felt nothing. Zip. Zero. Nada. It was what I would imagine kissing a warm fish would feel like. It wasn't really comfortable but wasn't uncomfortable either.

My impression of Tom's kiss might have been different if I had never had those incredible kisses from Eddie, but I did have those kisses from Eddie and I doubted there would ever be someone who would kiss me in a more passionate and 'entire' way than Eddie had.

There was nothing there when Tom kissed me, nothing at all, and I had absolutely no interest at all in kissing him again.

Tom and I stayed friends; we skated together when we were at the skatel and we hung out, but that was all that ever came of Tom. I would point out cute girls to him to let him know I didn't see that there was anything between us. He was completely friend-zoned. Eventually, he started seeing someone and I remember feeling very relieved.

Next was Steve.

Now Steve was sort of linked to the skating crowd too, just in a different way. Steve had a blondish short haircut in a business-type haircut and I can't remember much else about his appearance. There were a group of deaf guys at the skatel that were part of our extended group. One of my good friends was dating deaf guys. He was such a cutie. My friends and I began learning sign language. The deaf guys would teach us the swear words and phrases that we didn't learn in books, and we would also read the books that would teach us the formal way of signing.

I remember this one particular night at the skatel when my friend and her boyfriend were fighting. He was suddenly not so much of a cutie anymore and was being a bit of a jerk. Looking back now, it must have been quite a scene that night. My friend stood next to me, our other friends stood behind us. Her boyfriend and the rest of the deaf guys stood in front of us. I was yelling at him, telling him how much of a jerk he was while I was signing the words I knew. He may have been chuckling at me, who knows what I was really saying in sign language, but I let him have it. My voice was loud and my signing movements with my hands were tense and filled with anger.

By the end of the night, he and my friend had kissed and made up; they were probably having a real good laugh at how badly I had used sign language. Whatever reason it was that they made up, I was happy. If me making a fool of myself had helped them resolve things, then so be it.

Anyway, Steve. Steve was a hearing friend of the deaf guys. Sometimes we would leave the skatel and go driving with the guys in their panel van or other cars and just cruise around town. Steve had his own car and one night I ended up sitting next to him in the driver's seat. We got to talking and he asked me out, I said yes. We didn't really go on a date, we just hung out with his brother and a few of our mutual friends at his parent's house one afternoon. Steve asked me to go outside with him and we were walking around the yard. No hand-holding, nothing really sweet or romantic, just talking. After a while, we all went home.

Steve drove me home and when he pulled his car up out the front of my house, he leant across the front seat and he kissed me. It was a very purposeful move. There was no hesitation, no gradual lead-up to the kiss. He simply turned the car off, turned towards me, and planted one on me.

Now by this time, I'd had a few kisses from a few different guys and I was getting the idea that every guy kissed differently. Steve leant across the front seat of his car and planted a kiss on my mouth. Lips slightly open, a small amount of tongue; it was a bit blah but could have had potential with a few more practice runs; that is until he pulled away from me. As he moved back to his side of the car, there was a string of saliva connecting his mouth to mine. I could see it shimmering in the sunlight that shone through the windscreen. It was long and thin and just hung like a bridge between our mouths.

I shuddered on the inside. It was so gross. I'd pulled back and the string of saliva just got longer. Yuk. Ewwww. I'm shuddering now in disgust as I remember.

Needless to say, that was the last time I hung out on my own with Steve and it was definitely the last time we kissed.

Chapter 5
George, Again

Yep, that's right, we're back to George. You'd think I would have learnt my lesson the second, or the third, or maybe even the fourth time we had broken up, but nope. For some really stupid reason, I went back to George. His younger sister was one of my best friends and it turned out that I was seeing him all the time. I even had the privilege (cough cough cough) of being able to see him and his girlfriend being all over each other when I visited his sister at their house. It didn't bother me at the time, because I was doing what I was doing with the aforementioned guys. That should have been another sign of alarm bells for me to look at—I wasn't bothered by him smooching with his girlfriend, so I really shouldn't have bothered with being with him again.

At this point, he'd broken up with his girlfriend and we were both unattached and we got back together, again. This time, it was different though. We were both a bit older, a bit more experienced in the world of dating, and had different expectations of what we wanted from the relationship than what we had the first, second, or third time that we had dated. Could we really call it dated? Looking back, it was more a 'hung out together' kind of thing. George and I still hadn't been on a one-on-one date.

We were hanging out with friends most of the time, drinking and just being teenagers who weren't quite legally old enough to drink or go to pubs and clubs. Some of our friends were already in serious relationships and it seemed everyone around us was having sex. It wasn't something I felt pressured to do, nor was my first time with sex something that I was trying to get over and done with. But I am pretty sure that George was looking for any possible opportunity to do the deed.

His older sister had an apartment in town and we stayed there one night. This was going to be the night. It was our first sleepover. I had no idea what to expect. All I knew was that the first time would hurt a little bit.

I didn't know that when you had sex for the first time, for most people, it was very awkward. Now at the time, I had no idea what to expect, this was my first time and George had led me to believe that he was highly experienced in playing hide the sausage. It was many months later when he admitted to me that that first time for us had been his first time too. Considering how the first time had turned out, it would have probably been better for him to tell me the truth in the beginning, I might not have been so disappointed.

I may have dated or hung out with those guys before George, and while Eddie and I did a lot of serious kissing, I never had sex with him or anyone else. Apart from that last evening with Eddie when I was playing with his tally whacker and the other time of felt George's 'belt buckle' shaped erection against my hip the day I had turned 16, I had never had any sort of experience with that area of the male body.

I'd never been naked with a guy. I had nothing to compare it to the act of sex too.

Apart from some intense kissing, some fondling and a hand job, I had been innocent. No one had ever touched my vag-jay-jay unless it was over the top of my clothing, and the touching had only been bodies pressed together, a guy's hand had never been down there.

That first time with George wasn't overly pleasant or exciting. There was no skin-on-skin foreplay, there was no warmup of any kind. There were no long, sensual, tender kisses, no caresses, no touching each other. We decided we were going to go all the way and instantly he was ready to go and he didn't care if I was ready or not. He was eager to get his pecker into my fun zone and wasn't concerned about anything else. I guess for an 18-year-old guy to get ready for sex, all he has to do is think 'I'm going to have sex' and then his sex parts stand instantly at attention and he's ready and raring to go.

We got naked, the whole undressing part seemed to take longer than the rest of the entire act. Sex for the first time for me was a case of 'Ouch', 'That's feeling a bit better', and then 'Was that it?'. To be honest with you, I'm not even sure he was all the way in before he was finished.

After a few weeks with more practice, we got a little bit better at it and we both learnt the importance of making sure we were both ready to go before he slipped it in. It was so much more enjoyable if I was a bit wet down there then just him trying to shove himself in while I was dry. Remember, I did mention at the beginning of this story that I was very naïve. It's embarrassing to realise just how clueless I really was. When I was younger and Mum had given me a book to read that had all the info about sex in it, I had embarrassingly laughed and looked at the drawings instead of actually reading it. In hindsight, I should have read it, then I may have had some sort of clue about all this.

The first time he asked me to give him a blow job, I wasn't sure it was a real thing that people did. When I first heard the term 'blow job', I instantly thought that it was the guy getting a hair dryer to dry his shorts and curlies, and for the life of me, I couldn't figure out why they would like that. When George told me exactly what it was he wanted me to do, I figured I'd give it a go. He was fully hard before I got anywhere near it, and I swear all I did was breath on it and I was suddenly wearing a warm and sticky facemask. I hadn't even made contact and he was done.

Had I done it wrong? Had I done it right? Surely that can't be all there was to it? I didn't even do any of what he'd told me he wanted me to do. We cleaned ourselves up and that was that. 17-year-olds these days definitely know a lot more about sex than what I did back then. Looking back, it's scary how little I knew.

We'd left school by this stage and started hanging out with our friends who were all couples. After we were both 18 years old and legally became adults, we moved in together and started saving money to buy our own house. We would go out to clubs, movies, picnics, game nights and road trips. Apart from when we were driving in his car, George and I didn't do any outings alone. When the first of our friends fell pregnant and when the first baby in the group came along suddenly our world changed from nights out to dinners and clubs to doing game nights every Friday night at a different friend's house, BBQs, or other activities that were family-friendly.

As long as we were all hanging out and having a good laugh, it didn't really matter what we did and where we were. It just worked. It was comfortable. As we were hanging out in each other's houses, I never really needed to worry about dressing up, wearing heels, styling my hair and wearing makeup every day, which meant I was still the daggy, nerdy, plain old me I had always been.

The first of our friends got married and suddenly we realised we weren't teenagers anymore, we were in our early twenties and growing up fast. I'd left the community supermarket and gotten a job a one of the major hospitals in a customer service role. George scored himself a full-time job through his uncle and we began saving money. The school days were definitely behind us. We were in the real world now. It wasn't full of romance and rainbows but it wasn't too bad either. It was fun, comfortable and stable.

I will never forget when he proposed. It's not a story I was happy to share around when I was asked how he popped the big question. In my mind, a proposal should be something thoughtful, something planned, and something designed for the person who is being asked the question and there should always, always be a diamond to match the tastes of the person being asked. If you love the night sky, then the proposal should be under the stars; if you like the beach, then the magical question should be asked while you have sandy toes and salty hair.

If you like big parties and affairs and being the centre of attention, then the proposal should be in a public arena or around all of your family and friends; if you like lowkey and private, then the moment should be special and intimate; you get the drift. It should be something that has been well thought through, it should have words that are full of meaning and be spoken from the heart, and it should be planned to suit the person being asked the question.

My proposal was nothing like that, it wasn't special, and it wasn't designed just for me. To be honest with you, I don't know if he proposed on impulse or if he had actually planned to pop the question the way he did. Either way, it was a very poor effort. We were in our early to mid-twenties and we were lying in bed one morning, just waking each other up with some morning sex. We'd finished and we were both laying on our backs not saying anything, and he rolled his head to look at me. He said, "What do you think, should we get married?"

That was my proposal from George. No ring, no declarations of love, nothing.

Now you're probably thinking I'm a bit of an idiot at this point, and looking back at things now, I would have to agree with you. I was a huge idiot, one of the world's biggest. After all, George and I had kept breaking up and getting back together, we saw other people. I didn't know it then but he had become a comfort, a habit (I only realised this fact as I was writing this out) but I had thought I was totally in love. George gave me what all our friends had—a partner, a marriage and a promise of the house, the babies, and a happy ever after. It just seemed like that was what we were meant to do.

Now that I'm 45 years old and have been through some shit, I know a lot better. I know that a marriage proposal should have your heart skipping a beat, you should be emotional, and ecstatic. You should want to scream it to the world and you should show your ring off to anyone and everyone. You should not be left thinking 'WTF?'.

I wonder how Eddie proposed to his wife. I'd had no contact at all, I didn't know if he even was married. I just figured with the way he did the romance thing, he would have a very special someone. Probably best to not think about that.

Nope. None of the good stuff happened to me. Instead of asking where my diamond was, or suggesting he may want to plan the proposal and ask me again, I said, "Sure." He said, "Ok." And that was it. We got out of bed and got ready for the day ahead of us. The whole thing was so uninspired and unexciting that I can't even remember if this happened on a work day or a weekend.

There wasn't a ring, there was no emotion, there was no instant celebration. I don't remember how long after the proposal it was that we went in search of a ring, but I do remember that it wasn't too long after. We went out together to buy a ring and we ended up buying the whole bridal set because it was cheaper that way as there was a set on a great sale. The diamond was tiny but when the wedding band and eternity ring were added, it was a nice size.

The ring made it official. We were engaged.

Not long after this, one of the other couples in our group became engaged too. Her proposal had been magical. Her man had taken her away for the weekend. They'd gone out to dinner and after dinner, they'd gone for a walk through a park that had a waterway running through it. When they had gotten to the middle of the bridge over the water, he'd gotten down on one knee, held out a diamond ring, and proposed under the moon and stars.

I'd definitely been ripped off with my proposal. But I never complained to George about it, I just sucked it up and got on with life. I was very happy and excited for our friends, and I was a bit envious too.

My wedding to George was planned for 18 months' time and I had so much fun planning it. I had a ball. It was tricky keeping both families happy but I managed to pull it off. Organising the church that my mum insisted we get married in, the reception, the cake, the music, the dress, the photographer, the honeymoon, and everything else that needed to be planned and booked for the big day; it had all been fun. I had enjoyed it all. I was not a bridezilla by any means. When the bridesmaids and I had gone shopping for the dresses, we had the dress, shoes, and all bits and pieces chosen by lunch time.

On the day of the wedding, I had both my parents with me in the limo that was taking me to the church. The idea was to get to the church the long way and take a detour through town. I wanted to show off a bit and it would get me to the church about 5 mins late, it was tradition for the bride to be a bit late. That was the plan.

However, my mother wouldn't have a bar of this. The limo, which I had invested a small fortune in, drove the 3.1 kilometres straight to the church. When we got into the limo, I asked the driver to take the long way to the church and drive us through the main street of town. If we had done this, I would have been 5 minutes late, which would have been perfectly acceptable. But my mother argued with me. Trust me, when Mum got on a rant, it was just easier to give in to her wishes and keep her happy. We headed straight to the church. At least the guests saw me arriving in the limo, they were still arriving as the limo pulled up the driveway.

I could see George and the groomsmen get quickly ushered inside. That's how early I got to the church for my own wedding.

I must be the only bride in history who was standing at the door of the church welcoming her guests as they were still arriving.

The ceremony was done, the photos were done, and the reception was done. Everything had gone off without a hitch. I had a great time dancing, drinking, and being a princess for the night. I'd had that much of a good time that I told George he needed to divorce me so we could do the wedding thing all over again.

At the end of the night, we walked out of the reception under a guard of honour formed by our guests then George and I got into a limo and went to stay at a beachfront hotel for our wedding night before we jetted off on our honeymoon the next day.

The marriage seemed to be going ok. We had our ups and downs just like everyone did but we did ok. Life really wasn't any different to how it had been before, the only thing that had changed was my last name and I had an extra ring on my finger.

Just over a year into the marriage, we started trying to have babies.

I had been on the contraceptive pill since I had turned 16 and I was worried it would affect us being able to conceive. Before some of you judge me about being on the pill so young, my doctor suggested it as a remedy for the horrible time I was experiencing with my monthly cycle.

When I stopped taking the pill, my hormones went crazy. I broke out in acne across my cheeks and forehead, I was moody, my skin went oily, sleep seemed to be a hit, and miss exercise and weight bounced up and down for a while until my hormones rebalanced.

Twelve months after we had begun trying to conceive, we still weren't pregnant. I'd spoken to my doctor after about six months of not falling pregnant and he had told me that he would start fertility testing after the twelve months of unsuccessful trying had gone by. I didn't think we would actually get there, but here we were twelve months into unsuccessfully trying to fall pregnant.

I had been doing everything I could think of, and it had become very normal for me to lay on my back with my butt against the wall immediately after we had sex and rest my legs up the wall, just to make sure those little swimmers would swim up towards my ovaries and not down my legs towards my toes. I was reading books on how to fall pregnant, I was checking the calendar for that right time of the month to conceive, I ate different foods, I had a little Buddha statue near the bed for fertility, I locked my legs at the ankles around his waist as he'd cum to hold him in deep; maybe if I stopped him from pulling out, the little swimmers would swim deeper. I tried everything. Nothing was working; it looked like we needed to talk to the doctors about fertility testing and find out what options we had to help us fall pregnant.

Then it was winter time, we had both come down with the winter sniffles and we both felt like shit. We both called in sick at our work places and spent most of the day in bed coughing, spluttering, sleeping and snoring. But at some point through the day, we must have begun to feel better. Or maybe it was just that we were young, we had no one to look after, and we were stuck in a winter-fuelled, warm and toasty bed and nothing but a lazy day together. We woke up, we had the opportunity to do the hanky panky, and went back to sleep, thinking nothing more of it.

Several weeks later, I was one day late with my period. Now one day usually doesn't mean anything but for me it did. My cycle was always on time within a few-hour window. I could start the day with now worries and know that I'd have to insert a tampon at lunch time. Honest to god, since I began taking the contraceptive pill when I was 16 years old, I was spot on time within an hour or two every month. And now I was a day late. Could our tryst between the sheets when we were feeling sad and sorry for ourselves have done the trick? Do sperm get sick when the sperm owner gets sick or do they stay supercharged?

I went to the supermarket and bought a pregnancy test. As soon as I got back home, I peed on a stick and within minutes, two faint lines came up. We were pregnant!

The pregnancy was normal until the third trimester, then it wasn't really good. I gained a massive amount of weight, I had pre-eclampsia and was on forced bedrest for what seemed like forever. My ankles disappeared and if I crossed my ankles, I would develop canyons in my legs that looked deep enough to be a small bowl. It was horrible. My feet swelled so much that I was pushing my luck to get men's thongs on my feet. But we don't have much choice over what our hormones do when we are pregnant, do we?

I felt like a massive elephant with squishy legs and couldn't remember what my toes looked like and I felt like I was doing the overweight penguin wibble wobble waddle. I was strictly advised by my obstetrician to not do any exercise and to have nothing but bedrest, which did nothing to help my weight or my mental health, but I had to do what was best for the baby.

George was as supportive as he could be, and I do remember sitting on a chair in the bathroom as he shaved my legs for me in preparation for the big day. With all the health issues I was having with the pregnancy, I was obsessed with making sure I went into labour with freshly shaved legs. My legs should have been the least of my worries but they were my priority.

I had to have labour induced and baby 1 was bought into the world two weeks early due to dangerously high blood pressure. After induction, I was told I had to have an epidural to reduce my blood pressure.

What's that, doctor? You want me to have a spinal block and numb all pain from the waist down to help my baby? Sure, no worries! Get that horse needle into me and stop this contraction pain.

Baby wasn't really the healthiest when he appeared into the world twelve hours later but showed a fighting spirit from the very first breath and pulled through to be a healthy and happy baby, and just the most beautiful thing ever.

I loved being a mum and loved being on maternity leave and being able to spend time at home with the baby. George seemed to love coming home to baby and me. Having taken twelve months to fall pregnant the first time, we thought we would start trying for Baby 2 pretty quickly, and we unexpectedly fell pregnant pretty quickly too. Nineteen months after Baby 1 was born, Baby 2 came into the world.

And this time, things were a lot different.

The relationship between myself and George had begun to strain. I figured I was feeling these things due to pregnancy hormones and tried to figure out what it was that I was doing wrong to upset George. We really weren't expecting to have two babies under 2 at home. I managed ok, most of the time. Baby 2 didn't like to sleep much and I struggled to keep up with two babies, manage the house and do it all on about four to six hours of broken sleep each day. When he got home from work, George seemed to spend time with the babies but didn't interact much with me. He was working long hours, he didn't do much at home to help, unless it involved him spending time with the babies.

While he was playing with the babies, I would catch up on the housework I wasn't able to get done through the day. At the time, I was really happy with this arrangement.

I remember the community nurse dropping in for a visit to make sure I was coping ok, you know that standard home visit from a midwife/community nurse that got done when we took our babies home, well this was that. The day she came to check on me, the kitchen sink was overloaded with dirty dishes, there were toys, clothes, shoes and god knows what else all over the place. And I was a bit of a mess with my nightly sleep having become a few hours of broken sleep here and there. Baby 2 didn't seem to realise that sleep was something that people needed and would only sleep for an hour or so at a time which meant I didn't sleep much.

That nurse gave me some of the best advice I have ever been given. It didn't help me at the time but I did use it years later. She just sat with me and talked to me, asking me odd questions and reassuring me that I was doing a great job. During one conversation she told me that one day each school term, she and her child would play hooky from work and school and go out on a date day. They would go shopping, go to lunch, go to the movies, go to the park, anything that meant they would be spending quality time together. The hooky day was completely unplanned, which meant they were able to do whatever they wanted and wouldn't be interrupted. It was purely mum and child time.

As soon as she told me her amazing secret, I knew it was something that I would have to do with my babies too once they started school.

That is something for you to think about too. When my babies began school, I did do these 'hooky' days. It was the best thing I could have done. The babies finished high school a few years ago but they still brag about these hooky days.

Back to this amazing community nurse. After this particular visit, she said she would come back and visit me again in a couple of days. On her next visit, she was asking me what I thought were weird questions, but what she was doing was checking me for post-natal depression. Looking back, I did suffer from it for a bit, I'm sure of it. I never had it diagnosed though. I was lucky that I was only mild and it didn't last for too long. Now that there is more education and awareness of post-natal depression; I am more aware of the symptoms and I am confident I was experiencing it.

I am fully aware that the baby blues can affect women in different ways. For me, I remember everything being a struggle; it was like my mind was cloudy and fuzzy. I was running on autopilot and anything that I needed to concentrate on was too difficult to comprehend. I hadn't been living life day to day, I'd been living life hour to hour. Life had become mechanical and there was no enjoyment in it, mostly due to the exhaustion I was battling through on a daily basis.

I couldn't seem to get Baby 2 to stop crying. George would come home from work and spend time with the babies. I would use this time to do housework and prepare dinner. What I should have been doing was taking the time to sleep but I didn't. The chores needed to get done and they were something that I could complete without needing to concentrate on what I was doing. Apart from helping with the babies, George was no help at all and all the household chores were up to me. It didn't occur to me to ask the doctor for help, and when I finally did, we found out that Baby 2 suffered from reflux.

I tried the reflux drops, different formulas, and burping techniques but nothing seemed to work for the poor little baby. I began asking my mother for help and she was a godsend. She took Baby 2 for a couple of nights so I could get some sleep (Baby 1 had begun sleeping through the night at 3 months of age) and she helped me get Baby 2 into a sleeping pattern where he would sleep in one stretch for about four hours. George was completely useless and was no help at all. I found a way to get through the days of several hours of broken sleep each night and began to form a routine that would work for us.

George, Baby 1, Baby 2, and I settled into family life, and I thought we were doing ok.

I thought by pushing myself to my limits and doing everything I possibly could to make life easy for George, I was being a great wife and a great mother. But George interacted with me less and less, and I was so busy trying to do everything that I didn't make any effort to change that. George was good with the babies, and the only other things he would do when he was at home were eat and sleep. There really wasn't any affection, intimacy or even deep and meaningful conversations between us. And I hadn't noticed the lack of a 'relationship' with my husband. As I write this, I am remembering more and being aware of more about what was going on. I was exhausted and trying to do everything to make his life easy.

He was avoiding me.

Now, I am smart. I'm quite the nerd when it comes to academic things. But when it comes to life things, I can be very slow at adding 2 + 2 and getting 4. Up to this point in life, I would usually add 2 + 2 and get 524. This is why it took me so long to figure out what George had been doing.

By the time we had our two babies, mobile phones were a thing but they were nothing like the phones of today. We could make phone calls, send limited-length text messages, and play the 'Snake' game on our mobiles. There weren't any of the strict privacy settings or ways to hide things on your phone. George and I had matching little Nokia mobile phones. George was a truck driver and delivered products to a fast-food chain for their restaurants, and mostly used his phone for work purposes. Back in those days, we didn't live on our phones the way people do now, and we all still had landline phones as well.

One day while George was sleeping, his phone beeped. Now, back then, there were no passcodes to get in, there were no thumbprint or facial IDs required to unlock a phone, and if someone sent you a message, it was for a reason and not just to brag about what they were doing, or what they were eating or because they were bored. There were no social apps, it was just plain, old, boring text messages that were character-limited, phone calls and Snake; you couldn't even send a photo at this point. When George's phone beeped again not long after the first beep, I grabbed his phone to take it into him; two messages in a row must mean it was sort of urgent.

As I walked into the bedroom where he was sound asleep, I could see the message on the screen. There were no hiding notifications or any of the privacy settings we have now. Back then, the messages were on the screen for all to see.

The text message on George's phone read 'Hubby has found out about us'.

Chapter 6
George, the Asshole

Fill up the wine glasses, ladies, refresh the cheese platter and top up the crackers and grapes. Or better yet, get a dart board, attach a photo of an asshole that you have known in one of your relationships and throw darts at the board hitting the asshole right between the eyes (Not recommended to do this if you have kids running around the house). Poke out his eyeballs. Put holes in his smile, pierce craters in his cheeks. After all, the majority of us have known an asshole at least once in our lives, haven't we?

I asked George about the 'Hubby has found out about us' text. George's explanation of the message on his phone was to say that one of the girls at one of the restaurants he delivered to on his delivery run had been having problems with her husband and needed someone to talk to help her get through it all. Apparently, she had been using George as a sounding board to help her get through some tough times.

Here is another moment where you can feel free to call me an idiot. I had believed him. Every word and every lie he fed me, I just sat back and believed him. Before you start rolling your eyes at me—save the eye rolls for later—it gets worse. Not only does what George was doing get worse, but my stupidity and ignorance of what he was doing do too.

I praised him for being so thoughtful and considerate to someone in need. He smiled. It didn't occur to me to ask why she was talking to him and not to her female friends or her family. Where was her bestie? Why did she feel the need to talk to him? Another question I should have asked was exactly what kind of 'conversation' were they having.

Come to think of it, a good question for me to ask would have been 'Are you going to pack up your stuff or should I throw it out the door?'.

A week later, I asked him how she was doing with her husband, were things getting better? Had he been able to help her sort out her relationship at all?

George wasn't overly impressed that I had asked and again, I was in the bad books. He was frustrated with me again. I really had no clue what I had done wrong.

Yep, I was that dumb.

Not long after then, maybe three or four weeks, George was a few hours late home from work. Being the caring, considerate and amazing wife that I was, I rang him to make sure he was ok, after all, he drove a lot in his job and he worked long hours. Being late was normal for him, but only about an hour late and not more than that, and he always let me know when he was going to be late. It was perfectly reasonable for me to worry about him if he was several hours late home and I hadn't heard from him.

He didn't answer his phone when I rang but arrived home not long after and he was not impressed that I had become worried and tried to contact him. The guy drove trucks for a living, he worked long hours and had shifts that started in the wee hours of the morning and I was in trouble for worrying. I got into trouble for calling him and checking to see if he was ok. I think that was the first time I thought of him as an asshole. I was tired too but he didn't seem to notice.

Still, even though I knew something wasn't quite adding up, I tried to make it up to him by detailing his car for him; he always loved to have a spotlessly clean car. An immaculate car was his pride and joy. While cleaning the interior, I found some paper napkins like the ones you got in fast-food places and two of the napkins each had a different girl's name and phone number on them. Yet I still finished detailing his car.

"They are girls I work with," was his reply when I asked him about it. He flipped it off as no big deal. He took the napkins from me but didn't throw them away.

Again, I accepted his answer and didn't ask any further questions. It never occurred to me to ask him why their numbers were written down on napkins, or why he had hidden them in his car, or if they were contacts at work, why he hadn't saved their numbers into his phone.

Things remained tense between us. George's moods were very much up and down. After a few more weeks of walking around on eggshells and trying to figure out just where I was going wrong in the marriage, George told me that he was feeling a lot of pressure providing for the family and needed to have some time with his friends each week. He'd said that some of the guys he worked with were all catching up for coffee after work one day each week to just hang out and have some down time. I thought this was a great idea. At this point, I was happy for anything that would help make George feel better as this would improve the mood in the house too.

I was in control of the finances of the relationship. I sorted out all the money coming in and gave him some money each week for him to play with. I paid all the bills, did the groceries, made sure the boys had everything they needed, and added some funds to our savings each week. George mentioned he was running out of money each week so the next week I gave him some extra cash. He asked why, and I told him it was so he had money for coffee with his mates as he'd mentioned he was running out of play money. Again, he got cranky with me and for the life of me, I could not figure out what I was doing wrong.

How could I have gotten in the bad books for giving him more money to play with? I was turning my mind inside out and upside down trying to make sense of it all.

At this point, I had become stuck in the rut of allowing him to make me feel like I was the reason he needed time away from the family to relax with friends. I felt that I probably shouldn't pester him if he was late home and I felt responsible for him not having enough money to do what he wanted. My focus was on the babies and on keeping George happy, I had no idea I was losing myself in the process.

I was losing my identity, I did nothing for myself. Every moment of my life was consumed by the babies, George, the house and work. Losing your identity in any relationship is horrible. It happened to me without me even realising it. I was so focused on making sure that I was looking after those around me that I loved that I wasn't loving myself. Not that I am making any excuses for George's disgusting behaviours but if I had demanded time for myself for the gym or shopping, or just doing anything that was just for me, then maybe I wouldn't have lost myself. George would have definitely still been a complete asshole but I wouldn't have lost myself as I was learning that my husband was an asshole.

You do remember me saying before that I was an idiot? Just to clarify this to anyone in this position, you are not an idiot. You are being taken advantage of, you are being used, and the only things you are doing wrong are believing what the asshole is saying and changing things to try and keep the asshole happy.

George decided to spice up our sex life with a toy which he bought without telling me he was going to do this first. I found out when I walked into our bedroom and saw it laying on the bed. Remember in an earlier chapter when I told you I was naïve? Well, I had never seen sex toys before. I had heard about dildos and vibrators but thought that they were only something that was used in porn videos. George wanted to use them, and I wanted George happy, so I said yes. This also meant that we would begin having sex again.

When we got the knack of using the toys, I have to admit I enjoyed it, though I was way too embarrassed to use them without him. I finally worked up enough courage to tell him what I wanted him to do to me one night during a moment of passion and his response was, "Nah, I don't want to do that."

I was humiliated. It was the first time I had ever asked him to do something to me and after the instant rejection, I never asked him to do something to me again. I felt like a fool. Especially when I had never said no to anything he asked me to do to him.

By now you've figured out what was happening with George, haven't you? I won't continue on with all the boring details and the endless hints that I was ignoring as to what was going on and I'll skip straight to the point.

George was not happy in the marriage and he wanted out. He was also having an affair.

Suddenly, I was standing on that small patch of land that was just big enough for my feet. I felt like that land was tethering atop a really tall and thin column and I was wobbling over a bottomless abyss while torrential rain poured from the storm clouds above my head, tears cascaded from my eyes, mascara ran in black rivers down my face, and I just couldn't help but think what the fuck had just happened.

George left our home and slept on his sister's couch for a while. I had thought of trying to lure him back home with sex and it worked. Late one night, he began sending me text messages telling me he was horny. I encouraged him to come over to have a late-night romp between the sheets. In the back of my mind, I was thinking that if he came over and we had sex, he would come back to me. He would realise just how much he missed me and he would come back home. George came over and then he left straight away once we were finished. I quickly realised that sex was not the answer, and if anything, it did nothing but make me feel so much worse than I had before we'd had sex. What the hell was I doing?

On the following weekend, and I'll never forget this, he told me he was going to stay at a hotel to get a good night's sleep in a bed. I had thought that was fair, his sister had young kids and if he was sleeping on the couch, he wouldn't have gotten much rest or privacy.

Now my cousin who lives five hours away was visiting town that weekend for some sort of sporting event that was happening, and she happened to be staying at the same hotel as George had booked into. The next day, I was told this because my cousin had seen George with his arm around a young blonde's shoulder as they walked into a hotel room. Now, to add to my humiliation, it wasn't my cousin who told me. My cousin told her mum, who then told my mum, who then told me. So several people knew and I was the last one to find out. I guess that's the way these things happen though.

George came over that evening to see the babies and I tried to mask my feelings about what my mum had told me earlier that day. He was smiling, he was more amicable than he had previously been but he was still flirty with me too. Asshole. I kept busy doing odd chores around the house and bit my tongue. There was no way I was going to have this conversation in front of the babies.

I waited until the babies went to sleep and I confronted him. I stood directly in front of him, looked him right in the eye, and asked him if he'd been alone at the hotel. Without skipping a beat, without changing his facial expression or breaking eye contact he said yes, he'd been alone. I told him I'd heard he had been there with someone and he flatly denied it all while looking directly into my eyes and smiling. When I told him he had been seen with a blonde lady, that the person that had seen him was my cousin and that the news had gotten back to me, he said he had noticed my cousin but had tried to hide so she didn't see him.

And then he had the audacity to get mad at my cousin for telling on him. I asked him if it had made him feel like a big man, sleeping with two women and lying to us both. The asshole actually smiled at me and said that he had enjoyed it. It made him feel good, and yes, he had enjoyed it.

Every tiny little piece of any possible feeling of love, attachment, attraction, desire or any other nice, positive feeling I had previously felt towards him disintegrated and evaporated into nothing at that precise moment.

Double asshole. Triple asshole. A thousand times asshole.

It was then that I pictured what it would be like to murder someone. George and I were having this conversation in the kitchen, I was standing with my back to the cutlery draw. It wouldn't have been too hard to grab a carving knife out of the draw and accidentally slip, causing the blade to slice his cocky, arrogant, conceited, pompous, cheating, lying, asswipe, jerk, deceptive throat. That would get that evil smile off of his face. Asshole.

I don't remember what happened much after that though. I realised then and there that my marriage was 100% well and truly over. I was numb. Horrified. I was furious. I was desperately trying to figure out what I had done that was so wrong. I felt ashamed. Was I that bad of a person that my husband had to cheat on me? Why didn't he love me anymore? Had he truly loved me in the first place? Where had I gone so wrong?

Now when I look back on that time, 14 years after the fact, I realise that apart from being too trusting, too loving, too giving and trying too hard, I really hadn't done anything wrong. George was just scum. George was an asshole. George was the one who should have felt ashamed, not me. George was the one who should have been bending over backwards to try to keep me happy, not the other way around. George was the one who had cheated, who had destroyed our relationship and to help him deal with his guilt over his actions, he had been taking it out on me.

Asshole, asshole, asshole.

Over the coming months, George began to drop into the house at any time he chose. He wouldn't call to let me know he was coming, he wouldn't knock. He would just walk in and start going through things. I asked him to let me know when he was coming and he refused. He said it was his house too and he could do what he liked.

He even began taking things with him when he left. I'd worked to create a playroom out the back for the babies and I'd bought a brand new television with a built-in DVD player for the babies to watch their *Bob the Builder*, *Postman Pat*, *Thomas the Tank Engine*, and other DVDs that they loved. One day, he walked in, went to the playroom, picked up the TV and walked back through the house with that television. He walked straight past Baby 2. Baby 2 asked, "Where's Daddy taking my TV?"

Asshole daddy replied to Baby 2, who was only 3 years old, "Daddy has to get something out of this house." And he put the television into his car and drove it away.

I needed to put a stop to this. The police told me that while his name was on the mortgage, I was unable to stop him from entering the house at any time, and I also couldn't stop him from taking anything from the house. The only way to stop him was to get his name taken off the mortgage, which meant I had to buy him out. I couldn't afford to do that, I was only working part-time and I had no choice but to sell the house and move. I couldn't put up with him doing this. It was doing my head in and it wasn't fair to the babies or to me.

When I started to prepare to regain control and move on with my life, George started fighting back. He obviously didn't like that he couldn't control me anymore. He would come to the house and yell at me, pointing his finger at my face. When I started to cry, he would leave. It didn't matter if he was there for two hours, or thirty minutes, or ten minutes. After a week or so into this, I realised the pattern in what he was doing. It got to the point that as soon as I saw his car pull up out the front of the house, I would start crying. The quicker I cried, the quicker he left. Asshole.

Baby 1 was at preschool and it took me a couple of weeks to get the courage to tell Baby 1's teachers that their father had left the family home. The teacher's reply was unforgettable.

"We knew something had changed," she had told me. "But we never imagined his dad had left." Baby 1's artwork had become brighter and happier. He was socialising more with other kids and was more engaged in the preschool activities. His teacher told me they had never seen that kind of response in a child when a parent had left the home before. I had to work hard to get the courage to tell the teachers, I had felt so much shame at the fact that my husband had left. But it turns out, that the babies had been noticing more than I realised and that their father leaving the home hadn't had as much of a negative impact on them as I had thought it had.

This feedback gave me the courage to continue regaining control of my life and I put the house up for sale. That was the only way I could legally get George out of my life as much as I could. George didn't argue when I asked him to sign the paperwork to sell the house. Turns out, his desire to get money was greater than his need to control me.

I had a BBQ one night and invited some friends over. The babies were going to have a sleepover at my parent's house. George heard about this plan and came over through the day and took the BBQ with him so I couldn't use it that night to cook with. I shrugged my shoulders and cooked the meat in the kitchen. There's more than one way to BBQ. He came back later that night and parked his car across my driveway so the guests parked in the driveway and on the lawn couldn't use the driveway to leave. I threatened him with the police and he left but his car stayed where it was.

A few of us went for a drive, getting cars out by simply driving across the lawn and over the gutter, mostly so my friends could get me away from what he was doing. He started following us. He had left his car across the driveway and was the passenger in one of his friends' cars. Now he was getting his mates involved? A few days I arrived home to find him standing in my kitchen. He had started going through my rubbish bins looking for god knows what.

George became desperate to get me to give in to him and take him back. He must have had his head screwed on wrong if he thought his actions were making me miss him at all. One afternoon, he drove his new car around to my house and came to the door. He bragged about this car, it was a car I quite liked. He told me that if I took him back, he would give me the car. Looking out at the car, I asked him who was driving it as there was someone in the driver's seat. His girlfriend, the blonde girl he had been cheating on me with, the one my cousin had seen him with, was driving the car he was promising to give to me if I took him back then and there.

What type of asshole would stand at my front door and ask me to allow him to come home and bribe me by giving me the car that the girl he cheated on me with was sitting out the front of my house? George, that's who.

When I said no to his oh-so-generous offer, he was quick to tell me how nice it was to be sleeping with someone who was a size 10 in clothes and looked after herself. He turned around and walked back to the car without even saying hello to his babies.

George, the asshole.

Chapter 7
George and the Divorce

I realised I needed to get myself some 'rights' in this situation and I needed to make sure that I would be able to stop George from walking into the house at any time and helping himself to items from the house. I just couldn't afford to buy him out, that was not an option. I had no choice but to sell.

It took a few weeks to get paperwork sorted, legal bits and pieces, photos of the house and get the house officially listed on the market, but it didn't take too long to sell. Within two weeks, the house was under contract for sale and once we had a settlement date for the property to exchange hands and for me to be moved out. On hearing this news, George quickly packed up his belongings and took off to the other side of the country to live with a family member. He left me to sort out everything to complete the sale. It was a scummy move on his half, which I am pretty sure was designed to make me struggle and have me beg him to come back.

I wasn't going to do that and I think this is the time in my life when I started to become stubbornly independent. George may have felt he was punishing me by making me do everything myself but he had no idea what I was capable of. I was now a single mother of two babies, I had a good job, I had a great family, and some incredible friends. There would be no stopping me. I was becoming stronger, I was becoming empowered. I didn't need him, I didn't need his help. I was going to do this without him. And I was going to do an amazing job with it all.

I sold the furniture and bits and pieces that I didn't need from the house. I registered with the Child Support Agency to get child support payments from George and when George found out, he was not impressed at all. How dare I make him pay me money to help cover the cost of raising our children? He believed he shouldn't have to do that. He even rang the Child Support Agency and told them I didn't deserve any of his money. Ha! Asshole. A few months later, he realised those types of comments were listed in our file and the team at the Child Support Agency really didn't like him. His arrogance really wasn't doing him any favours.

I found a new-ish three-bedroom townhouse in the next suburb that was available for rent and the babies and I moved in. Before things had turned to shit and George had moved out, we would each read a bedtime story to one of the babies at bedtime, he would be with Baby 1 and I would be with Baby 2. Both babies would go to bed at the same time and we read to one baby each. You get the idea. Now, I was one parent and two babies. I knew all the warnings about not putting the kids in bed with you, that the babies wouldn't go to sleep on their own and all that, but these babies were my babies. They were my life.

One day they wouldn't want to snuggle with me anymore. So each night, the three of us would climb into my bed, with me in the middle with a baby on each side. I would read a story or we would snuggle and watch TV until the babies both fell asleep. Once they were out for the night, I'd carry them into their own beds and I'd go back to my bed and go to sleep for the night. This system worked, it was great. I cherished my snuggle time with them and they looked forward to bedtime too. They would each lay on their sides facing me, one of my arms around each of them and their heads nestled on my shoulders with one arm across my tummy while they fell asleep.

It was a win all around. I loved it. To this day, they still remember that; they had loved it too. My snuggle time with my babies had become my favourite time of day.

I soon got into a good routine and began to really enjoy being a single mum. I didn't have to answer to anyone, the babies and I could do whatever we wanted. The babies were smiling a lot more, they were happier too.

I applied for a divorce and got the paperwork started. Again, George wasn't impressed that I had done this, it seemed he was still waiting for me to ask him to come back home. I was beginning to think the asshole was delusional. To try to get back at me for having the audacity to apply for a divorce, he told me I was banned from hanging out with my good friend, his sister. Ah, no. Sorry asshole, you cannot dictate to me who I do and don't spend my time with.

When George would call to talk to the babies, now aged 3 and 5, I would give the babies the phone and do my best to ignore him, which turned out to be quite easy. I really had no interest in him at all.

I had begun to see a relationship counsellor as part of the divorce process. I tried to not feel any shame or embarrassment as I sat there talking to the counsellor and answering his questions. I think it was only the second meeting that I had with the counsellor when he stood up, walked over to his whiteboard, grabbed a marker, and started writing words on the whiteboard. Words like narcissist and manipulation. Then he asked me if I understood what the different types of abuse were and that was the first time I was shown the Cycle of Abuse Wheel.

I looked at him like he was crazy. This was the first time I had come across the word narcissist, I had no idea what it meant. I told the counsellor that George didn't abuse me, after all, he had never laid a hand on me. The counsellor then went on to explain the other forms of abuse to me. Mental, emotional, financial, social; it was all new to me, I hadn't had a clue about any of it. He also told me that it was his recommendation that there was to be no attempt at reconciling and if I wanted a good future for myself and my babies, I needed to go through with the divorce.

I told him about what Baby 1's preschool teacher had said when I told her that George had left. The counsellor explained how that backed up what he was telling me about the different forms of abuse.

The counsellor asked about the babies' artwork. Would I be able to bring some examples to our next session? He wanted to see what kind of drawings the babies were doing. I had no idea why but I was happy to show off the babies' creative skills.

I pulled a piece of paper out of my bag and showed him a drawing Baby 1 had done at preschool. I really loved this drawing, it bought me great joy to see the drawing. Baby 1 had drawn a huge rainbow over the page. Under the rainbow stood a very tall stick figure of me, next to me was Baby 1, then Baby 2. Baby 1 was angled towards me. The three of us had big smiles on our faces. I had thought the drawing was beautiful and bright and I had planned on doing the 'proud mum' thing and showing my mum when I picked the babies up from her after my appointment, this is why I had it with me.

The counsellor interpreted the drawing and told me that the drawing signifies that Baby 1 was very happy. He said Baby 1 had drawn me to be so big, and had myself and both the babies leaning into each other because I made him feel safe, and because he saw me as being everything he needed. Tears began to gush over my cheeks; it turns out I wasn't failing my babies after all.

There was never a thought of possibly fixing things with George after that. Not that I really wanted too, but there were times when I questioned whether I was doing the best thing for the babies by divorcing their dad. I guess that was a thought that most separating parents go through at least once in the divorce process.

George never once attended a counselling appointment. With the custody part of the divorce process, he refused to show up to meetings or respond to phone calls. All the appointments had been created to be done remotely taking into consideration that George was at that time living in a different state and with the ability to have the meeting via teleconference.

Again, the asshole probably thought he was making things difficult for me my not cooperating. Again, he had just made it easier for me. The mediators gave me a special certificate which indicated that he had refused to participate. This certificate meant that the judge would approve whatever custody arrangements I wanted. I decided to wait a little while before I had formal custody arrangements put in place. George was living on the other side of the country and hadn't seen the babies for a couple of months.

He may have felt like he was controlling my social life by not allowing me any free time but I didn't want any free time, I just wanted my babies. And if something came up where I would need to have the babies looked after by someone else, I always had my family close by to help.

Anyway, several months after my babies and I had set up our new lives and had become happy, George decided to come back to our side of the country. Somehow, he'd gotten the idea that I was going to give him another chance. What a delusional asshole.

Ah, excuse me? No chance in hell, sunshine. He then moved into his girlfriend's place, which happened to be about 500m down the road from where we lived. I wonder if it was karma that had her believing that he had been faithful to her while he had been living away from her in a different time zone. He'd cheated with her on me, what's to say he wasn't cheating on her while he was away for so long?

I remember about 2 years after this period of my life, George's girlfriend was feeling quite threatened by me. I found that quite funny. She was the same girl he had been cheating on me with when he left the marriage. I rang her and told her that there was no way I would ever have any interest at all in getting anywhere near close to George. I assured her if the human race depended on George and I having more children, the human race would die out.

I only tried to reassure her of this as she was living with George and when the babies went to spend time with George, she was there too. I didn't want her telling the babies anything bad about me, and I felt that assuring her I had no interest in George that this may help her.

She also tried to tell me that she felt I had concerns about her spending time with my babies and that I was threatened by her. I laughed so hard, I almost chocked on that one. I told her that my bond and my relationship with my babies was strong and full of love and happiness and that I knew that no one would be able to come anywhere close to getting between me and my babies. She never accused me of feeling threatened by her again.

It's true, I didn't like someone else having a caring role in my babies' lives but I had a wonderful relationship with my babies, I had no concerns about our bond being threatened as I was safe and secure in just how strong our bond was. I did, however, take the opportunity to tell her that if she ever hurt a hair on either of my babies' heads, I would be after her, and I warned her that there would be nowhere on the planet that she would be able to hide from me. I would find her.

Come to think of it, I'm pretty sure she didn't talk to me again after that. Lucky me. I can't give the girlfriend too much of a hard time though. When George had the babies overnight, the girlfriend was the one who looked after them and made sure they had everything they needed. I never told her I was grateful for that, perhaps I should have? Who knows?

One afternoon when George came over to see the babies, he told me I looked good. "So this is what I had to do to make you look after yourself?" He added. I smiled and thanked him through clenched teeth and walked away. I had lost about 10 kilograms. In my mind, I was thinking about how I'd managed to get rid of all the feelings I'd had for him, and once I was no longer miserable and became happy again, I just naturally lost the weight I'd been carrying in the marriage. What made me even happier was his little girlfriend was starting to gain weight. A lot of weight. The little skinny thing that he'd bragged about being with—to my face mind you—had gotten bigger than I ever was.

She reminded me of one of the characters in a cartoon the babies liked to watch. The cartoon character was a big ball that had short little arms and legs. Maybe he was the problem? (Insert evil laugh here) After all, he was the common denominator here.

George would come over one or two afternoons a week to take the babies out for an hour or so. Now, as sad as this is, I'm quite proud (and I know it's wrong but I am sure most single parents with asshole exes would feel my joy here) of how my babies played their dad. More often than not, he would pick them up, they would get him to buy them ice cream or some McDonalds, and then they would ask to come straight back home. Sometimes the kids were only gone 20 minutes. Kids are so smart. Still, I wasn't ready to enforce formal custody arrangements yet and George only wanted a couple of afternoons each week.

To get the divorce, we needed to be separated for twelve months then I could submit the paperwork. George refused to cooperate with this process; again he thought he was making something difficult for me, perhaps punishing me for not doing what he wanted me to do. The ironic thing here is that as he made me submit a sole application for divorce instead of a joint application, I didn't have to pay any fees due to the benefits I was on as a single mum. His 'punishment' of me had saved me the hundreds and hundreds of dollars I would have needed to pay had we made a joint application.

On the official day of the divorce case, I went to the Family Law Court, I was directed to a court room filled with people doing the same thing I was. George never showed up, naturally.

The judge called my name, I stood at the front of the room at the small table with a microphone on it, I felt professional and proud as I placed my folder with my copies of the paperwork on the shiny desktop. The judge asked me a question (I can't remember what it was), and I replied with 'Yes, Your Honour', the judge stamped his paper and declared the divorce would be final one month and one day from that day.

Once George received his divorce certificate, he told me that as I had divorced him, I didn't have the right to keep his surname. I did tell you I thought he was delusional, didn't I? The asshole seemed to believe he had the right to tell me what I could and couldn't do, still! But this demand seemed to sit quite ok with me. Why would I want the surname of a lying, cheating, manipulative, delusional asshole who put more effort into hurting and trying to control me than he did with his relationship with his babies? I changed my surname back to my maiden name, and it was so easy to do. I had set aside a few days to get the process done but it really only took me a few hours.

I took my birth, marriage and divorce certificates to the Roads and Traffic Authority and the lovely lady behind the counter even gave me a partial refund on my registration after she took my photo for my new licence (this was due to being a single parent on benefits). I took my new photo identification to Centrelink to change my name for my single-parent benefits and child support; I changed my name with Medicare; I went to the bank and ordered a new bank card. I logged into my works system and changed my name there, and voila! I was done. And it was wonderful! George felt he had won on that point but I was the true winner.

I felt empowered, I felt strong, I felt like I was taking back control of my life. I was 32, a divorcee, a single mum of two amazing babies, and I was ready to conquer the world.

Chapter 8
Greg, the Rebound

This is a really, really short chapter. (Maybe a short and skinny chapter would be more appropriate, you'll see what I mean.)

This was about four or five months after George had moved out and before the divorce was final.

Now the thing about rebounds is they are usually with people who have no chance in hell of a future with you. The rebounds are usually people that you can easily cut ties with, but at the time of meeting the rebound, we don't normally realise that the whole relationship idea with them is a lost cause. Greg was definitely rebound-only material.

I was still working, I had a part-time job and my mum was helping me with the babies while I worked. She would get Baby 1 to school, Baby 2 to and from preschool and I'd pick Baby 2 up from mum on my way home from work. Mum was an amazing support.

Work was with a medical service and we had a courier driver. I was in the back room this one day, talking to a fellow staff member about our work when the new courier driver came in through the back door. Greg had a head full of brown curls, had deep brown eyes, and wore thin-framed glasses. He had a deep voice, a slender frame, and it turns out he was very cocky (but not in the ways where being cocky would count).

We were talking for a few minutes when he wrote his number down on a piece of scrap paper, gave it to me, and then he leant across the bench we were standing at and kissed me.

What the hell?

I ran out of the office and rang my cousin straight away. "What should I do?" I asked her.

"Are you really asking me that?" She'd replied, "Get him to come over when the babies are with George and get yourself laid!"

It was a bit harder than just getting Greg to come to my house so I could get laid. Greg wanted to date. While I had absolutely no clue what I was doing, I went along with it. He was telling me how there was a tennis court in his backyard next to the inground pool. I called bullshit but he insisted it was true and one day a few weeks later, he took me to his house.

When we got to his house, there was in fact a half tennis court in the backyard next to the inground pool. There was also a caravan in the carport. It was his parents' caravan. "You store it here for them?" I asked.

"No," he replied, "I live with them."

Uh ohhhh. Warning! Warning! I could picture the red beacon light flashing in my head. This wasn't good, but then if all I was doing was having some sex, did that whole part about a man in his early thirties living with his parents really matter? Hmmm, I still don't have a clear-cut answer on that one. Life doesn't always go to plan and people have financial struggles. But still, I struggled with it. I had two babies to support and I was able to be on my own and support myself. Anyway, back to the story.

His parents had gone away for a couple of days and he invited me over this particular afternoon; the babies were with George so I went. He kept talking about his sexual prowess, how endowed he was, how incredible he was in the sack, how sparks flew when he went to work blah, blah, blah.

Now, before I tell you about how he was in this area, let me tell you; no, let me warn you. If a guy brags about the size of his package and how well he can use it, run! Run like the wind! Run like Speedy Gonzales and high-tail it outta there! This experience taught me that the more he brags about what he has, the less he actually has and the worse he is at using it.

Greg took me into his bedroom and we sat on his single bed (Yes, it just gets worse and worse). Now we all know what a zooper doper looks like, don't we? The long, skinny ice block encased in plastic that is all the rage every summer? That was Greg's pecker. He was a small version of a zooper doper. For those of you who haven't seen a zooper doper before, the ice block is about 2.5 cm in diameter, skinny and easy to snap between your hands. His pecker was so skinny and tiny, that I remember wondering where the rest of it was. Surely if he got more excited, there would be more to his, uh, length or girth?

Well, the answer to that was no. I tried all the tricks I had learnt (which wasn't many but I still gave it a go) but there was no way short of a penis enlargement that that thing would be a usable size. My extended middle finger would almost be the same size as his so-called package.

Greg was sweet enough some of the time but the sex was horrible, I'm not even sure it could be called sex. So definitely not worth the rebound. This is when I should have invested in a really good vibrator instead of a rebound. At least the only issue with a vibrator would have been the batteries going flat.

I gave him more than one chance to really perform, to prove that he believed the saying, it wasn't what you had but what you did with it. But no. It just did not get any better.

One day, we were swimming in the pool, his parents were out for the day, and he was getting very touchy-feely in the pool. The water seemed to make a bit of difference, so I figured I'd give him another chance.

I should not have done that.

We were upstairs in his room, on his single bed, bodies still wet and cold from the pool. His zooper doper penis was ready and raring to go. I was laying underneath him and his nose began to drip, the drips falling on my face.

While he was moving, thrusting the skinny and short penis in and out, he mumbled, "My nose drips after I've been swimming," and he just kept doing his thing till he was done.

It was disgusting. I feel like dry retching just remembering it. Insert massive cringing shudder here. Ewwwww. Yuk, yuk, yuk! I was being snot dripped on while a tiny penis barely touched the sides of my vag-jay-jay.

Greg became very clingy very quickly and began looking at me with puppy dog eyes whenever we were together. He started buying me jewellery which I couldn't accept knowing that I was about to give him his marching orders. It seemed the more obvious it became that I wasn't into him, the clingier he got.

Then he did something so disgusting that I had wiped it from my memory. He had done this many times before but it took me a while to actually realise what it was that he was really doing.

I was chatting with my cousin the other day and she asked how I was doing during the whole break up with Luke. I told her how I was doing this writing therapy to help get me through this time, and I gave her a brief rundown of the guys I had already written about. When I mentioned Greg, she dry retched and she reminded me of Greg's horrible act. As is the dripping nose while having sex wasn't bad enough, I was reminded about how he would put one of his hands down the back of his underwear, I can only guess that he was rubbing his butt hole, and then he put his fingers to his nose and sniffed them. I'm really dry retching now! Yuk, gross, vomit, ewww, no, no no!

He didn't last too long (and yes, that refers to in bed as well as in this book and in my life).

Bye-Bye, Greg, the Rebound.

Luke Update! Luke had been waiting for something to be delivered to our/my house. It is a certificate for a course that he completed earlier this year.

I sent him a message to tell him the certificate was here. What the hell is wrong with me? I am still cranky with him but I am also starting to feel terrified again that I have lost him. Part of me is still sure that we will get back together but I also know that is going to take time. I am impatient and I don't want to wait. I just wish he would talk to me. He hasn't addressed the message I sent him two nights ago. Maybe I didn't win that argument. I feel like shit.

The pub where he is staying while he is away for work is open again; the Covid lockdown is over in that region. What if he met someone and was talking to them? But if he was doing that, he wouldn't be online, would he? What if he is talking to some woman online? It kills me to think that but I can't do anything about it. My imagination is most definitely not my friend.

I am really fighting against sending him another message. I just don't know what to do.

I'm going to grab some tissues, have a cry, and I'll be back soon to continue my story.

Chapter 9
Kent, the Worst Life Lesson

Yes, readers, the worst life lesson. Now you may think how could things get worse after cheating George? Or even after finger sniffing, nose dripping Greg? Surely that could never happen?

Well, as we all know, never say never.

Just a heads up, the Kent part of my story isn't that good. I probably should have mentioned this at the beginning but I have changed the names of the guys in all of these chapters. The reason I chose the name Kent for this particular guy is the name is very close sounding to the Cee You Next Tuesday swear word. A very good friend pointed that out to me, and considering the type of guy Kent turned out to be, the name is very apt.

*Apologies to all the guys out there named Kent. I hope you're all nice and wonderful men. I acknowledge that there are nice 'Kents' in the world. This Kent just wasn't one of them.

Now, onto Kent.

Kent was one of the neighbours in the townhouse complex the babies and I moved into when I sold the house as part of the process of stopping George from helping himself to the home and everything that was in it, as well as trying to control me.

I used to sit on the little front area of my townhouse and watch as the babies would ride their little trike bikes in circles across the little porch area that was level with the ground, down the driveway. Kent would get home from his work in the afternoons after the kids were home from school and I was home from work. I was lucky with my job; I worked about four hours a day and was home with the babies every afternoon.

Kent would nod hello if he saw me. Up to this point, I had tried to keep to myself. I had been in the townhouse now for about six months and didn't know any of the neighbours by name. To be honest with you, I sort of liked it that way.

I had just wanted to focus on my babies and I was happy to not have the neighbourly chit-chat when I was out in the front.

Kent was a smidgen shorter than me, he had dark brown/blackish hair, a goatee and brown eyes. He had a slightly rough appearance and I couldn't help but think of a bad boy when I saw him.

He had a motor bike in his garage. I remember hearing him revving the bike in his garage and I was curious. I grabbed the bag of rubbish out of my kitchen garbage bin and walked past his townhouse to the garbage bins that were kept in the middle of the townhouse complex so I could have a sticky beak inside. He had been revving up the bike, smoke billowing around, while a woman, who seemed to be in her early to mid-twenties, videoed him.

I can't remember exactly how we started talking, but I think it was when he knocked on my door one day to let me know about a party they were having. I wasn't getting invited, he was just letting me know to expect some noise.

We got to talking and it just grew from there. The first time he kissed me was nice, it was a bit of a thrill. He kissed me with confidence and I liked it.

Looking back on things now, I realise that we didn't really date, we just started hanging out together and hanging out together began to happen more and more often. We would spend a lot of time with other people whenever we were out and about. There were always groups of people around. I just became included in his plans.

After a while, I met his family, he met mine. My babies seemed to like him; he was familiar to them as they saw him every afternoon when they were riding their trikes out the front on the driveway. His kids seemed to like me, there weren't really any objections from anyone. It seemed to flow quite naturally.

Kent's sister lived overseas, and we'd been together for about nine months before he went overseas to visit her. I dropped him off at the airport. I was emotional, he was emotional. It was what you would expect. We had been seeing each other every day and now he was going overseas. From memory, he went for close to two weeks. He rang me via video call several times while he was away. When he got home from his trip abroad, he declared his undying love for me, he got down on one knee, held a diamond ring up to me that he had purchased while he was away and proposed. I besottingly said yes and he, still on his knees, wrapped his arms around my thighs and almost cried with happiness.

Then he stood up, put the diamond ring on my finger, and we danced. He twirled me around the kitchen and lounge room. We couldn't stop smiling and laughing.

A couple of months later, Kent was asked by his employer to relocate to a suburb about two hours away for work; he spoke to me about it and asked my thoughts on it. He considered what I said and together we decided to make the move. I told my parents, they were happy. I told George, he didn't say anything. Once I had relocated away, he began to have the babies from a Friday night to a Sunday night every second weekend. We did half the travel each, and it took a long time for George to realise that with these arrangements, he got to spend more time with the babies than what he was spending with the babies when we lived in the same area. It was incredibly hard for me to get used to George having the babies every second weekend for the whole weekend.

I found a place for us to move to and Kent moved into the new place before the babies and I did to start work at the new site. The babies and I followed up about two weeks later. We moved into the house and set everything up, the hire truck had been returned, all boxes had been unpacked, and we'd ordered pizza for dinner as we were both completely knackered.

When the pizza arrived, Kent grabbed the box, threw it across the kitchen, and started yelling at me. I had no idea where it had come from. I stood there, rooted to the spot, watching as this man whom I thought I knew, turned into a stranger before my eyes and screamed at me. Then he just stopped, he walked upstairs, and he went to bed. The one-sided argument was over almost as fast as it had begun.

I put it all down to the stress of moving.

His temper didn't really show its ugly head again for quite some time. We'd been in the new rental house for between six to twelve months, I can't remember exactly, and we looked at buying a house. We found a house in a nearby suburb and moved again. The kids were all excited as the new house had a cubby house and an inground pool. It was an older-style house with high ceilings and large rooms. We did some small renovations, fixed the house up a little bit, and had lots of pool parties.

Then things started to change. It seemed to come without warning. There may have been warning signs coming, but if there were, then I didn't see them at the time. Looking back now, I guess there were plenty of warning signs, I had just kept making excuses for him when he snapped.

Kent's temper became fierce and it appeared quite often. His eyes would change, he'd get crazy eyes. I still don't understand how someone's eyes can change so much that they don't even look familiar. By looking at his eyes, I could tell if he had snapped. And nothing I could do would calm him down. Nothing. I quickly learnt to just get out of his way.

Now I can't remember the order the events happened but I do remember things that happened and to be honest with you, I am sure there are things that I have forgotten. If there is something I have forgotten, I really don't want to remember it. There are reasons why we block things out of our minds. I'm going to share with you some of the things I remember but I'm not going to dig deep enough in my memory to resurrect the things I've buried in there.

This chapter is the hardest chapter in the book for me to write. But I need to write it. I could spend so much time writing so many pages for the Kent chapters but I don't think I will. I'll give you the details but I won't dwell on them too much. And I will only tell you what I remember without delving too deeply into this horrible time of my life.

And please, please, if any of this chapter seems familiar to your situation, please get help. You can leave, you can move on, you can start again. No matter what these guys tell you, you are a wonderful person, you are loved, and you do have friends who will help you.

Now, let me share some details with you about the worst part of my life.

This particular afternoon, we had some friends over. This was at the house we had purchased. We were entertaining some of his friends in the back area of the house when Kent left the area and not long after, I heard water running. The house we had bought was old and you could hear the water running through the pipes throughout the house whenever someone was running a bath or a shower. I went to see what was happening and Kent was sitting fully clothed in the bath, running himself a bath in the ensuite. There were bubbles everywhere. He was sitting low with his head under water, his arms on the side of the bath holding himself down. He was trying to drown himself.

I yelled at him to come up out of the water but his hands just clutched at the side of the bath. I couldn't get him to come up for air, so I grabbed a handful of his hair and reefed him up. He looked at me with such crazy eyes, his eyes weren't his own. Even the colour of his irises had changed to a more intense and brighter brown; it was as though there was a fire on either side of his pupils which were tiny little pin holes in his eyes. "What'd you do that for?" He growled at me, then opened his mouth and went back under water. I didn't know if he was playing or not but it wasn't funny. I should have just let him go but I didn't. I ended up finding the plug and pulling it so the water would drain out of the bath.

He wasn't impressed. I went back out to his friends, hoping someone would be able to make some sense of what had just happened, but they couldn't. Not long after, they made their excuses and left.

Another day I got home from work and the crazy eyes were back. He'd gone through my bedroom drawers while I was at work and found my diary that I had kept when I was in high school. Now, lots of people used to keep diaries, especially those of us who like to write. I'd been keeping diaries for as long as I can remember. Diaries were a safe place to write your innermost thoughts and trust no one would see them, providing you hid your diary.

Now I wasn't keeping a diary while I was with Kent but I did still have my diaries from my high school days. These diaries were 15–20 years old when Kent found them. If you remember from earlier in my story, you'll know I met George while I was still in high school and naturally, I wrote about those days. Kent found these diaries and read them. When I got home, he confronted me about them. I had no idea what his issue was but turns out, he firmly believed I would read those diaries while he wasn't home and I would get myself off on reading about 15–16-year-old me dating guys for the first time.

It was purely coincidental that the diaries and the vibrator he'd bought me were kept in the same draw. But he wouldn't believe that. In his mind, I was using the sex toy while I read my diaries. How I was supposed to bring myself to orgasm by reading schoolgirl crush writing such as 'I walked past him in the hall today' or 'I swear he looked my way at lunch today', or writing about the horrid arguments I used to have with my mum. You see, I mostly only wrote in the diaries while I was crushing on someone. If I was actually going out with them, I tended to stop writing because I would just simply daydream instead.

Kent refused point blank to give me back my diaries and walked around with one in each of his cargo pants pockets for the next few days. The diaries were those small little hard back ones with little padlocks on them. At random points throughout the next few days, he would start reading entries out form my diaries, didn't matter to him who was around to hear him, or if we were inside the house or outside of the house, he would read out my entries real loud. The entries were all completely harmless but were what my innermost thoughts had been when I was a teenager and it was humiliating to hear him read out my words.

The most intimacy I experienced at that time was a kiss. But according to Kent, they were the worst and most disrespectful, horrendous acts that I could have possibly done and still owning the diaries was the utmost form of betrayal. The diary saga ended with him tearing them apart, page by page, and burning them in the backyard while he forced me to watch. Then he destroyed the vibrator he'd bought me.

Another time we argued and towards the end of the argument, I had to take the babies to one of their after-school activities, so the babies and I left the house to do that. When we got home, Kent wasn't there. We'd already had our dinner before we went to do the activity, so once we got home, the babies showered, brushed their teeth and then went to bed. After I'd said good night to the babies, I went into the kitchen and noticed the big container that we kept all our medicines in was on the kitchen bench. The container usually stayed in a high cupboard in the kitchen, out of reach from the kids.

I went to look at the container and noticed there were all these pill packets that were empty strewn across the benchtop. Kent was on some medication to help with mental health and all the tablets he had for the entire month's supply were gone but the empty packets were left behind along with empty packets of paracetamols and other tablets.

Before I go any further, I will tell you that I supported Kent through the mental health diagnosis that he received. I remember telling my cousin that if Kent had cancer, I wouldn't have left him, it wouldn't have been his fault he got the disease and I felt that what he was diagnosed with was a disease, and was not his fault that he had a mental illness. That would be true; except for the fact that Kent was borderline genius and he was using the diagnosis to get away with a lot of things, including what he was doing to me. He had also been a heavy drug user in his earlier days and this had begun to affect his brain.

I rang his mobile to see where he was and if he was ok. He answered the phone and told me that he was going to take all the pills and drive into a tree or a pole somewhere. I panicked. It was night time, I didn't know what to do. I'd never had any experience with any of this and just didn't know what to do. He hung up on me. I rang him back and begged him to come home. I begged him to tell me where he was. He wouldn't. He hung up again. I rang him back and threatened to call the police and for him to tell me where he was. He hung up on me. I rang him back and got cranky with him and told him I was going to call his mother. Not long after, he came home.

I can't remember ever seeing all those tablets after he got home and I don't know what he did with them. But he walked in the front door and went to bed, just as if nothing had happened.

Another time we were watching television and I got a message on my mobile phone. I went to check the message and that was enough to set him off completely. We argued for hours after that. He accused me of seeing someone else, of keeping secrets from him, he accused me of everything you can imagine. Even me showing him my phone and the harmless message that had come from a female friend didn't stop him. After that, I made sure my phone was always on silent after dinner time. If I ever forgot and I got a text message, he would lose his shit.

He started chatting to women online through a few sites. The sites he was on weren't dating sites, but they were sites where you could meet people and form new friendships. He seemed to only be meeting women and was spending way too much time on these sites.

One night, I'd cooked a roast dinner for us all and there was cauliflower on his plate. This particular night, he decided he didn't really like cauliflower and threw it at me from across the room.

One night time, we were arguing and he put his clothes in garbage bags and into his car, and he left. He left the front door wide open and just drove away. It took me almost an hour to get the courage to get up and shut the door. He came back the next day but kept his clothes in the garbage bags for several more days before he gradually began bringing them back inside.

I began losing a lot of weight, very quickly. I hadn't noticed this was happening until my shorts began to slip down on my hips. I realised then that there were days that I was so focused on keeping the peace that I just wouldn't eat.

Another time we argued, and to punish me, Kent forwarded his mobile phone to my mobile phone. Every time I tried to call him, I would get my own voicemail.

Before I go any further, I just want to say a few things here to defend myself a little bit. By this time, I was well and truly sucked into an abusive relationship, far worse than what my marriage had been. I am a person who has a very soft heart; I always try to help people, I always believe the best in people and I don't like to give up or fail. I can't explain how he did it but Kent had me walking on eggshells. He had me doing everything I could to try and make him happy and not once at any point during this time did I think that he was just a complete and total asshole who was abusing me. It's something that is really difficult to explain.

Unless you've been in that situation, you simply cannot begin to comprehend just how bad it is mentally. To contradict myself with what I just said, if I had had a stronger mindset, if I had realised exactly what was going on, then I simply would have cut all ties and walked away. But somehow, with whatever it was he was doing, I couldn't get my mind into that headspace I needed it to be in to leave.

When I figured out I was in a bad abusive relationship, things just got worse, or maybe they just seemed to get worse because I was becoming aware of exactly what it was that he was doing. If I did talk back or argue in any way, he would snap. Some days all I had to do was look at him in the wrong way and he would snap. I found myself wishing the babies' dad would come and take them away. I was ashamed. I felt so completely alone and had no idea where to go for help. I remember talking to my cousin who told me if I didn't leave him right then and there, she wouldn't talk to me until I did leave him.

I knew she was right but I couldn't do it. I don't know why but I just couldn't bring myself to leave. I felt restricted, alone, and isolated. I was broke, I wasn't sleeping, I wasn't eating. I didn't know what to do.

I was definitely standing on that small patch of land that was just big enough for one of my feet, trying to keep my balance while that land was tethering atop a really tall thin column, and I was wobbling over a bottomless abyss while torrential rain pours from the storm clouds above my head, tears cascaded from my eyes, mascara runs in black rivers down my face and I just couldn't help but think what the fuck has just happened. And that feeling stayed with me for a long time.

There was a period of about a week where he had put all of his clothes in the car again and threatened to leave. I told him to go. He didn't. But he kept his clothes in the car and if he showered or needed fresh clothes, he would go and get them from his car.

He would leave to go to work early in the morning, or he would take off through the night to go for a drive and leave the front door wide open, but also left me too scared to get up and close it. I always did get up to close it but I was terrified he would come back and yell at me for doing it. He would say he was going to get his medicine from an all-night pharmacy. Years later, the truth came out—he was picking up prostitutes.

At night when I would say goodnight to the babies, I would find myself apologising for the position I had gotten us into.

I still have a photo on my computer that is a hole in the wall. Not very many people know that the hole in the wall was from where he pushed me through it. I only ever got a bruise once, and that was under my chin when he picked me up by the neck of my jumper and held me off the floor while he screamed abuse into my face.

Sex became something that would calm him down. I no longer enjoyed it but looked at it as a way to calm him down and get a few hours of sleep. I hated my life and had no idea what to do about it.

One day, I was driving somewhere and sharp pains began in my tummy. I had the babies in the car with me. I managed to get back home but the pains kept coming and going. I started spotting blood, which was unusual for me. The next day, I made myself a doctor's appointment. The doctor said he believed I'd had a miscarriage. A miscarriage? I didn't even know I was pregnant. The pain lasted about another day, and once I knew what it was, I was grateful for every cramp and every scream my body gave me. To this day, I feel bad at how relieved I was to be going through that.

Not many people know about that. I think there's maybe one or two people that knew. I didn't even tell him about it. But my relief and joy at going through something that was so incredibly horrific and painful made me realise more than ever that I had to get out of the relationship.

Dear readers, unless you have been in this situation, there is no way I can explain the feeling of helplessness and being alone. The situation doesn't make any sense to you, you believe all the crap the assholes tell you, and you feel isolated. You truly believe there is no way out.

If you are reading this and you are in a situation like this, then please play close attention to this part: Whatever the asshole is telling you is not true. Your true friends are there waiting to help you, your family will help you, and there are professional services waiting to help you. Go to the police, go to the local hospital or medical centre, go to your kids' school; just go somewhere there are people that can offer help and tell them you need help. There is help available— housing, financial, counselling. There are services that will help you plan your escape, they will help support you to find employment and rebuild your life.

One night when the babies were with their dad, the shit really hit the fan. I can't remember too many details, all I know is it got really bad and I rang the police. They came to the house in two police cars, five police officers in total, and they were wearing fighting gloves and padded vests. He stood up to them, calling them names, and taking aim at them with his fists. He pushed one of them up and onto the wall. I was standing on the front lawn howling in fear, I was terrified over what I had done.

A police office was standing next to me trying to help me. I remember seeing the torch beams flying around on the other side of the window as the police needed to use their torches to defend themselves against him. There was one of him and five of them. That's how strong he was when he snapped. It took five police officers to restrain him. I saw bodies flying around the room. I could hear punches and grunts. And I was screaming and howling with each sound.

This is so hard to remember. I really hope things I have buried from this period of my life don't resurface. But if they do, I will deal with them.

I have no memory of him being taken away in the police car. I have absolutely no clue what I did the rest of that night. I don't know if I went to my cousins or if I stayed at home. I honestly can't tell you. I can't even remember how long he was in custody, or when he came home or what it was like when he came home. I can't remember if I slept, and I can't remember cleaning the scuff marks from the police officer's shoes off my walls, at shoulder height mind you. I do remember, ashamedly, that we did live together for a bit after that event had happened.

There were more things that happened but I don't think I'll get into any more. I think you get the idea. It was hell.

Chapter 10
Ending It, Leaving and Moving On

This chapter isn't really about a guy I dated but it's about how I left and moved on from Kent. I think it's very important to be able to tell this part of my story. I will never know just who is reading this and if there is the smallest possibility that I can write about how I left and how I picked my life back up and someone who is also in an abusive situation reads it and is able to get the courage to leave, then this chapter will be so very worthwhile. Please, if you are in a situation like this, know and believe that you can leave and you can start over.

Kent and I were still together after the arrest. Somehow he managed to convince me that it was all his mental health disease and I ended up testifying in court to help him. I was shitting myself. I was shaking, I felt sick. I had no idea what was happening. I was still standing on that small patch of land struggling to not fall into the abyss. This time, though, that small patch of grass was in a courtroom before a judge.

Kent's lawyer was very good at what he did. It was a closed court, just the prosecution and the defence lawyers, the judge, Kent and myself. I testified, that the judge ruled in Kent's favour citing mental health issues and demanded Kent seek professional help. We went home.

I had begun to picture in my mind how I would leave our home. I had planned the escape to coincide with Kent being away and coming home to us going. I just needed to get the money to do it. Kent kept me broke. My friends were still there for me but they were at a distance (understandably and if any of my friends are reading this, I love you to the moon and back and will always be grateful to you for still being there for me when I got through this time). My parents and sister lived over two hours away, I was alone. While I was planning the great escape, I just didn't know when it would happen. But I did know that I was ready.

Being 'ready' to leave is so important. You must be mentally strong enough to leave and deal with the anger that the guy throws at you and stay strong enough to not give in and go back to him. If you do go back, then it will be near impossible to ever leave again. You must be ready to leave in heart, in soul and in mind; the mind part is so important. When you leave, he will always blame you. He will always tell you how much he loves you, how you misunderstood, how he wants to make it up to you. You need to ignore all of it and keep walking. Do not look back. No matter how much you want to leave, you have to be strong enough to go. You have to be ready.

And I was ready.

The day of my great escape was a Thursday. How I remember these details, I will never know. I was in the kitchen cooking chicken schnitzels for everyone for dinner. It wasn't yet dark, the kids were all happily playing in their room and Kent came out to the kitchen to talk to me about something while I was cooking.

He insisted that he'd had a conversation with me throughout the day, which he hadn't as I'd been at work all day. I figured out that the conversation had actually been had with this ex but he was still convinced it had been with me.

There was no argument, there were no threats. We had a disagreement and discussion. There was no yelling but something inside me changed.

The best way I can explain is that it was like a switch was flipped inside my head. I turned the stove off, left the pan of schnitzels as they were, wiped my hand on a tea towel, looked Kent straight in the eyes and told him I was leaving.

I walked into the babies' room (I will always call them my babies but at this point, they were aged about 7 and 9 years old), told them we were leaving, and to pack some toys that they really wanted over the next few days into their school bags. I grabbed our travel bags and some plastic garbage bags and filled them with all the clothes and personal items I could. Kent was staying away from me and mumbling to himself in a different room. I guess he knew I was done. Or perhaps he thought I was joking. I filled the car as much as I could with what I needed to take for the babies and then some things for myself.

I went to him and told him if he damaged any of my babies or my remaining things, I would have him charged for damages and I would be back to get what was mine when I found a place of my own.

The babies and I got into the car and we drove away. It had been surprisingly easy to do.

As I was driving, I rang my cousin and told her I had left. She told me where her spare key to her house was and said she should be home about the same time we got there.

I lifted the floormat under the driver's seat of the car and grabbed the money I had been hiding there. I used it to put petrol in my car and we drove to my cousins.

My cousin was my angel. My babies played with her babies, they were so happy. At the time I felt for sure that they had to be aware of what had been going on. They knew that Kent and I were arguing, but the really bad stuff never happened while they were home, only when they were away. Actually, Kent pushed me through the wall when they were home but they thought I'd fallen. My cousin sat with me all night talking to me until I couldn't keep my eyes open. She later told me she did that so I wouldn't contact Kent. She had been helping me stay strong.

My cousin gave my babies and me a place to stay while I figured out our next step. She asked for nothing in return except for me to pick my life up and move forward and not contact Kent.

I had Fridays off, I was only working Monday-Thursday. When I took the babies to school the next morning, which was a Friday, I requested an urgent meeting with both of their teachers. I sat in the office and faced the teachers, took a deep breath and briefly told them what had happened. I told them we had escaped and were now in a safe place. I told the teachers I was worried about the babies and assured the babies that they were able to talk to their teachers if anything was worrying them. The teachers were a great support for my kids.

The following Wednesday I was working on a site visit at a charity organisation's office. The charity was an organisation that provides help to community members for financial aid, legal assistance, and advice; they have seniors groups, offer clothing and food, and among many other incredible things the charity did for the community, they also have assistance for domestic violence. My work went to this particular charity office every week, and once a month, I was included in the team that would visit the office to see clients.

This particular day, I had a client not show up for their appointment, so to pass the time, I was reading the flyers on the info board in the waiting area. There was a flyer for a place for women who were victims of domestic violence. Without knowing why, I reached out and picked up the flyer and went back into the office I used when I was there and began to read the flyer.

The lady who managed the centre came into the office and said, "If you don't mind me asking, why did you grab that particular flyer?"

I started crying and told her I had recently 'left'. By the end of the day, she had set me up with a counsellor and I had an appointment at the women's refuge place, though I didn't know what benefit I would get from the appointment. It felt like I was running on autopilot, yet I didn't know where I was headed. People seemed to be guiding me in the direction I needed to be in, and the direction that I wanted to be in. I went to the appointment at the women's refuge centre and I don't know how they did it, but between my cousin and the counsellor, I managed to not look back and began rebuilding my life.

Within a couple of weeks, I applied for a townhouse rental property. The application needed a previous rental history. I briefly explained my situation and why I didn't have an immediate rental history. I was expecting to not get the property but the universe was definitely on my side. The landlord of the property worked with victims of domestic violence. My application was approved.

I asked my parents to help me with the bond, I didn't have the six weeks' rent in advance. They did. I took the boys to school. My amazing cousin and her boyfriend helped me move all the furniture. I really don't remember packing up my things—there is a lot that happened over that period of time that I don't remember—and I don't want to. I'm not sure if that's a good thing or a bad thing.

For the furniture that I needed, I went to the Op shops (charity shops) and bought cheap used pieces. I had quite the eclectic look going. The boys had their own beds and all their toys and clothes from the old place but we didn't have any other furniture.

At work, we got paid quarterly bonuses if we met or exceeded our targets for the quarter. For that first quarter, and the following quarters for the few years following, the bonus would be spent solely on the babies. They would come home from a weekend with their dad and find new bookshelves, new quilt covers, an X-box, new bikes, anything they had been wishing for and I was able to provide. I felt I needed to do this to make up for all the crap I'd put them through.

After I left Kent, I found out that he was unfaithful to me many, many times with women of all ages. He would go to parks a night time to participate in 'dogging'. He would tell me that he needed to wind down and driving around at night time helped him wind down. I believed him. He hadn't been driving to relax, he'd been driving to pick up random women and have sex. I have no idea what else he was getting up to and I didn't want to know.

I made an appointment with my doctor and requested a full blood test including all STDs. My doctor was wonderful and asked me if I would like a mental health care plan so I could access counselling. I told him that I had accessed counselling through a different service. Thankfully, the blood tests all came back clear.

I would booby-trap the townhouse each night after the babies had gone to sleep. I'd put Lego blocks on the floor where there were windows; I put dowel rods in the window tracks so the windows couldn't be slid open; I'd move a lounge or a heavy piece of furniture to block the front door. I did this for months—no one would be getting into our place without me hearing them. Kent came to the townhouse one night and stood in the driveway calling me a slut and yelling out loud enough for the while street to hear. I rang the police. I can't remember how he found out where I was living.

I know I didn't tell him. Had he been following me? I don't know. He had also been sending me unsavoury text messages and unsolicited dick pics. I went to the police for help.

There was an apprehended violence order in place and he wasn't allowed to come anywhere near me or the babies. Thank god, they weren't his kids. The police confirmed that Kent had been issued with his papers for the order and then the police came to my townhouse to explain everything to me. While the officers and I were sitting at my dining table, Kent tried to call me on my mobile. The officers took of photo of his attempted call and went to arrest him. As he had breached the apprehended violence order, I did not need to go to court.

The total charges against him had him looking at several years in gaol. Somewhere along the line, some of the i's hadn't been dotted nor the t's crossed legally and he escaped gaol time but the apprehended violence order stayed in place.

I never saw him again. But he was watching me. The police advised me to move, change my phone number, change the babies' school, and get a new place of employment.

By this stage, I was stronger. I didn't do any of what the police had suggested. I wasn't going to let that bully control me any longer by forcing me to change my life.

I decided then and there that I had two choices. I could allow the fear of him to turn me into a recluse and hide away from the world, or I could ignore him and move on with my life.

I chose to ignore him. It wasn't easy but I did it. I didn't realise how good I had done until I received a phone call the following year on my birthday.

"Happy birthday," the male voice had said.

"Thanks, but who is this?" I'd replied.

"It's Kent," he said. I hung up the phone and realised I'd forgotten the sound of his voice. I smiled at how far I had come. I blocked the number he had called me from. It was actually a wonderful birthday present because I realised he didn't have the power to rattle me or threaten me anymore.

That was 10 years ago. Every now and then, he pops up somewhere on social media. He used to create new profiles and when they popped up, I just blocked him. I also blocked his friends that I knew. Just last year, the wife of his best friend tried to connect with me online, but I blocked her instantly. There have been times when he has tried to make contact with one of my closest friends on her social media and tried to get her attention. She just lets me know and blocks him.

Leaving a situation like the one I was in is up there with the hardest things I have ever done in my life. The process leading up to leaving was a complete mind fuck. I was ashamed, I blamed myself. I was broke, I felt alone, I felt guilty, I felt I deserved what I was getting. After all, that's what he had been trying to drum into my head. I learnt that I had no reason to feel ashamed, he was the one who was wrong, not me. With every day that passed after I left, I got stronger and stronger. I began to live my life for me. I was no longer ashamed. I was not a victim. I was a survivor.

Sometimes when I see people argue in the streets, I feel threatened; if people act in any way that reminds me of what Kent would act like, I would go into flight or fright mode. After some training in emotional intelligence, I know that the technical term for flight or fright mode is an amygdala hijack. I still do react that way sometimes, I can react in a way that doesn't make sense to anyone but myself. I don't know if I will ever get past that; though, it is happening less and less. Over the last few years, I have found myself speaking up for people who haven't yet found their voice because I remember what it felt like to lose mine.

But on the other side of that, I react to things in a way that's not really reasonable. While writing this out, I am learning how I have carried that past trauma into my current life. I'm not proud of that but know that I am aware of it, I can begin to heal that. I'll add more on this later.

If you know someone who is in a similar situation to what I was in, please understand this. It is oh-so very easy to say to someone 'Just leave', or 'You must want to be there because you're not leaving', or to say. 'It's not that hard, just pack a bag and walk out the door.' But for the person who is in that situation, they are the worst possible things you can say. Even though I knew these things were true when they were said to me, they were making me feel worse, because I knew they were true but I was too weak to act on it. Feeling worse didn't help me get the strength to leave.

The guys that do these things to women have us believing we are worthless, that no one cares for us, that we can't do things on our own, and that we are no good. When we keep getting told what we have to do, it doesn't allow us to build strength, and while your intentions are good, dictating to us what to do, or telling us that you can't understand why it's so hard for us to leave only makes us retreat back into a comfort area of what we know. And unfortunately, as horrible as it sounds—and as horrible as it is—those guys and the way they treat us is our comfort. Because when they are angry, we know exactly where we stand.

When he was happy and 'normal', I began to fear the real him coming out. The longer he was happy, the worse he got. I wasn't able to enjoy the normal days, I was constantly walking on eggshells trying to not upset him and living in fear of when he would get angry again. It was a horrible, twisted, mind fuck of a situation that was complete and total hell.

What would be helpful, if you are trying to help someone in this situation, is just simply letting the person know you love them, that you are there for them when they are ready to leave, reminding them of their strength and awesomeness, and giving gentle encouragement.

I can't stress this enough, it is very hard to explain, but unless you have been in that situation (and I pray to the universe and the gods and anything else that is out there that you haven't), you just can't understand how hard it really is. It is possible, it is doable, and when she is ready to leave, she won't go back. But it is really, really hard.

After leaving Kent, I was a different person. But then, how could you go through an experience like that and come out the other side the same person you were when you went in?

I was now more sceptical, I asked more questions about situations and people, I didn't smile as much as I used to, and I kept to myself more than I ever had before. My circle of friends had shrunk drastically and I liked it that way. I learnt all about privacy settings for social media platforms. I didn't go out much, I stayed home and kept to myself and the babies. I guess you could say that the wall of protection I had around myself was now as tall as a castle's walls and there were crocodiles in the mote surrounding it. There were no knights in shining armour trying to lower the drawbridge, and I was more than happy with that.

I had no intention of ever being in another relationship again. My ex-husband had cheated on me and then Kent had abused me in more than one way. If I were to believe what the counsellor had told me about George, then George and Kent were very similar in how they took advantage of me. George never put his hands on me but I was now aware of what mental games he had been playing with me. Both of them had tried to control me, and at times, I was letting them control me because that made them happy. They both took their guilt out on me, they both did everything in their power to deaden my spirit, to dull my sparkle, to stop me from being me.

I was determined to not let that happen ever again. I would get my sparkle back, I would get my spirit back. I would rise from the ashes stronger, brighter, louder and larger than before; they were not going to win in their crusades to destroy me. It would take me time but just watch. I would rise again. Nothing was going to stop me from living my life and creating as good a life as I could for my babies.

Reach for the stars readers, and when you get to the stars, keep going. There is so much out there for you, you just need to go and get it.

Ok, I got the really shitty relationship out of the way. Let's get back to some more normal stuff.

Chapter 11
Justin, Todd and James, the Ego Boosters

Ok, before I tell you the details about these guys, I just have to say, I've just had another freaky Friday moment (and it is Friday too!). My cousin just sent me a link to a video on Facebook. I checked it, it's a video clip of prominent Australian female singers performing the song *I am Woman* by Helen Reddy. I had just written the part of the last chapter telling you how I would rebuild and rise again. How's that for timing? Right at the end of the Kent chapters too. Girl power baby! *'I am woman hear me roar…'*

On to the Ego Boosters.

Now if you haven't figured it out by now, I don't have a lot of confidence in myself, even less now after Kent. I still consider myself to be average and I am still oblivious to guys paying me attention. And to be honest, after my experiences, I wasn't sure if I did want any attention from anyone. My ex-husband cheated on me, and after I was able to figure out his patterns, I realised he had done is at least three or four times; it wasn't just once with that last girl that I had met. That girl who sent him a text saying that her hubby had found out about him was another woman he'd been sleeping with. So were the two girls' names on napkins that I found in his car. There were probably more women too.

I'll never know. And to tell you the truth, where I was at this point in my life, I didn't really care. George may have changed my outlook on love and marriage, but the one thing I knew for sure was that I no longer had any feelings towards him at all. I didn't really care what he did as long as it didn't impact the babies. I didn't love him, I didn't hate him either. There was just nothing. And having no feelings whatsoever towards him was wonderfully empowering.

One of the ladies in my office used to tell us girls that the best thing you can do after a breakup to get over a guy is to get under a new guy, preferably on a one-night stand with a guy who you wouldn't want any more than a one night stand with. I didn't agree with this. For some people, it might work, but for me, it doesn't. If others want to go out and have one-night stands, then I take my hat off to you. Have a great time, and remember if it's not on, it's not on. (There's nothing wrong with the woman supplying the condoms either! Just make sure you use one! Or if you're really lucky, two or three.)

I don't believe in myself doing that, and to this day, I have never had a one-night stand. It's not the type of thing that would sit well with me, but I do understand that some women can do this and it works for them. No judgement here, it's just not my scene. Even though the time I had spent with Kent had changed me, it hadn't changed me that much. At times I wished I could do it but I just didn't have it in me.

My cousin was also keen for me to get out there and just have sex. By this time, I was in my mid-30s and I had never had a one-night stand. It was frustrating to have my cousin and workmates telling me to go and just have sex, I really didn't want to and they couldn't understand that. They had my best intentions at heart but they seemed relentless with their suggestions. I gave up arguing with them about it but I didn't do it, and even though I stopped telling them 'No, I don't want to', I was proud that I stood my ground and didn't do it.

I'm not sure how long it took for this part of my life to happen, it would have been at least twelve months after I had left Kent. Whatever the timeframe was, the next step for me was Justin. Justin was about a foot taller than me, with dark hair and brown eyes. He worked out at the local gym several times a week and he watched his diet. He had a glorious six-pack, loved wearing muscle tops that showed off his sculpted arms, and there were always girls in their young 20s hanging around him. Justin was 23.

I met Justin after George and I divorced. We were just friends, I really hadn't thought any more about his friendship and interest because he was 12 years younger than me (And don't forget, I heavily lacked self-confidence).

The first time Justin sent me a flirty message, I replied by asking if he realised that he had sent that message to me and asked who the new lucky girl in his life was.

He'd replied saying he had meant to send it to me. I laughed at him and told him he was crazy.

He ignored me and kept sending messages. I asked him if I was some game to him. I asked why he was sending me these messages.

He replied by telling me that he had always thought I was gorgeous and sexy and asked me why I thought he would always come and talk to me when he saw me.

"Because we are friends?" was my reply.

Apparently, it was more than friendship to poor Justin. Justin had a crush on me and was lusting after me badly. All he wanted to do was to get me into bed and show me all the things he had imagined doing to me.

Then the flirty messages changed into more intensely raunchy messages. Some of the messages he sent me made me blush but it was exciting too. I had no idea how to respond to some of the messages, and I think that encouraged Justin to continue sending me very detailed descriptions of what he wanted to do to me to give me the most powerful orgasms he was sure I would ever experience.

And I'll be honest here, readers, if I had a vibrator at this point in my life (I'd still not had the courage to get myself one after George and Kent), I'm pretty sure I would have used it and orgasmed just thinking about what Justin was saying to me while that little magical toy was happily humming away down below.

I weighed up my options. I was single. He was single. There would be no chance in hell of anything serious happening, it would only be a fling. His words indicated that he knew what to do. Was I old enough to be a cougar? Imagine knowing I could get a guy 12 years younger than me into my bed. He had a beautiful body from what I had seen. He lived a couple of hours away, what would be the chances of him seeing me anyway? It would probably just be a few sexy text messages and then he'd get bored and leave me alone.

But what if he did come and visit? Would I be ok with never seeing him again afterwards? It could be a bit of fun. Could I do this? What if he was actually able to deliver on his words?

A glass of wine or three later, my answer was clear.

Yes, yes, I could.

I googled the term cougar to see if I would in fact be one, and I was right on the cusp of it. I was just under twelve months after being classified as a cougar. That made me feel a bit better.

The next time he sent me a flirty text, I replied with a flirty one of my own. Justin tested the water with some sexy messages and I encouraged him to continue. Over the following days, the messages turned into XXX-rated messages that had my skin tingling and my lady garden ready to go into full bloom.

I hadn't even seen him and my confidence was already growing. I knew I wasn't doing anything wrong but it didn't really feel that right either. As my confidence was growing from all the attention he was giving me, I decided it really wasn't a bad thing after all. What did I have to lose? I might learn a thing or two (wink-wink).

Finally, the day came when he sent me a text and asked if he could come see me. After I recovered from a small panic attack, I said yes, after all the boys were away, so this mouse could play. It was weird seeing him in the flesh while my mind was going through all the things he had said he wanted to do to me.

Would it be rude if I just skipped the hello and the catch-up and just threw him onto my bed instead? I really struggled with what to say. I could feel myself blushing as I remembered the words that I had read. He seemed to pick up on my nerves, or perhaps he just had the same idea and began to kiss me. I remembered what kissing 20-something guys was like when I was that age. It was obvious this 23-year-old knew a hell of a lot more about kissing than those other guys had known and all my doubts seemed to disappear.

He walked me into the bedroom all the while kissing me very thoroughly and taking my clothes off as we walked. It was amazing, I hadn't had that happen before. Turns out, he knew a bit more about a lot of other things too. This guy definitely knew what to do. While what he had written in the text messages was pretty amazing, his actions were so much better than his words. He made me feel so desirable, so sexy. My confidence grew and grew and grew with each orgasm. There were definitely no regrets about having a bit of fun with Justin. No regrets at all.

We met up a few more times for more fun and then I called a stop to it.

To this day, I still don't know if he was a toy boy or not, but if I were ever to talk about him, I would more than likely refer to him as one, especially now I'm in my 40s. It sounds good to say 'I had a toy boy'. I will also be forever grateful for how he made me feel. My confidence skyrocketed; I felt sexy, I felt like every woman should feel. I learnt a few things too (insert a very big, cheeky smile here). There were many days after Justin and I first had sex that I never thought of Kent or George at all. It was really a great way for me to begin moving on with my life.

I never saw or heard from Justin again after I called it quits, but I do hope that he knows how much he did for my self-confidence.

Ego boosted.

Now on to Todd. Todd was a very spiritual man. He was a reiki Master, he had brown hair that shone with orange highlights in the sun, was the same height as me and had brown eyes. (Are you noticing the pattern here with brown eyes? Everyone has had brown eyes except for George!)

He was also a man who I could just not ever be in a relationship with. He was easy to talk to and easy to spend time with, but I couldn't see myself doing more than that. We had similar spiritual beliefs but other than that, we had nothing in common except a mutual acquaintance. He was a bit of a traveller, very nomadic, the feeling that he emitted made people feel that he would forever be single and would never commit to anyone or anything except for the open road. He had commitment issues and he wanted to travel for the rest of his life.

He was a free spirit and he was never going to be tied down to the one spot. He was very happy-go-lucky, very much carefree, very much not the type to settle down and commit to a relationship.

We met through a mutual acquaintance, and there was nothing in our meeting at all—there were no sparks flying, no love at first site. He was just a person who seemed like a nice guy, who was a friend of someone I casually knew, someone who was easy to talk to. He spoke of things I didn't really understand; he wasn't being arrogant or pretentious, his world was just completely different to mine. Even though I didn't fully understand the things he was talking about, the things he spoke of interested me. I have a very curious mind and am always keen to learn about things I know nothing about. Todd would explain things to me and answer my questions without making me feel silly or inadequate.

We had both been at several of the same parties or get-togethers and we were at one particular function when he and I had a conversation that was a bit more personal and to the point than all the other ones had been. He told me that he had felt drawn to me from the very first time he'd met me and that each time he had seen me after that, the pull he felt towards me had gotten stronger. I really didn't buy too much into his line. I didn't think too much of it other than it was his standard pick-up line.

Using similar logic to what I had used when I was wondering what I should do with Justin, I just decided I should just go with the flow and see what happens.

After all, George had been the only man I had ever been with before we divorced; I had lost time and experiences to make up for.

We were standing around the corner from everyone else at the party, in a dark and private corner when he held me close and looked deep into my eyes asking if I could feel the heated pull between us.

I said, "Huh?" I had no idea what he was going on about.

He explained that he could feel a hot pull, like a magnetic force between us, in the solar plexus regions of our bodies (just under our tummies). He had his hands on my hips, he was looking deep into my eyes, and our bodies were moving slowly in rhythm but not quite touching.

I said yes, there was a warmth that I could feel. Mind you, this warmth could have just been the fact that he was standing close enough to me for our clothing to be as close to touching as possible without actually touching. It could also have been the fact that what was happening right at that moment was quite intense. The eye contact, the gentle unison sway of our bodies, his hands on my hips, I was definitely warming up and I could definitely feel a heat between us, which was weird considering there had been no previous chemistry. Maybe we just hadn't stood close enough for the solar plexus magnetic forces to connect.

According to Todd, this solar plexus chakra was responsible for helping with confidence, self-esteem and feeling in control of my life. I figured I needed those things. He was sort of cute, I wasn't repulsed when he pulled me in for a nice, tight hug. So I played along and let him continue to feed me lines. To be completely honest, I was enjoying it too. It was like a different type of foreplay, and it was definitely working.

He maintained eye contact, he was talking softly in a low, deep voice and his hands were so warm on my hips, that I could feel the heat of his touch searing the skin under my clothing. He leant in and placed his forehead on mine, our heads slightly bent downwards, our eyes closed. Our breathing was deep and slow. Our bodies continued to sway in unison, our fun parts coming close to touching but not actually touching. Our bodies began to sway in larger circles, our clothes began to brush; a sway or two later, our sacral chakras (the ones that govern the sex organs) were brushing against each other in the swaying movements. Our sacral chakras were on fire.

While our bodies still danced together, he leant forward and kissed my throat chakra. The contact of his lips on my skin changed the small spot fire he had started within me into a stormy wildfire. Sounds of pleasure escaped my mouth,

I was shocked at the primitive sound that came from me. After he nuzzled my neck, he moved his mouth to mine and kissed me in a slow and deep kiss, his tongue tasting mine and his lips moulding against mine. It was the most erotic moment I have ever had while still being fully dressed.

We moved our dance to the bedroom and before too long, he had all my chakras shining and glowing and singing in unison. After we'd finished, he told me to stay still and he held his hands over my body. He told me he was performing reiki on me. I didn't even know what reiki was, but as Todd told me about the energies he was healing within my body, I swear I could feel the heat and movement of his hand which was hovering a couple of inches over my skin. Even with my eyes closed, I could feel exactly what part of my body his hand was hovering over.

Another time the group of people we both hung around were going camping and we were both going too. No one knew that we had united our chakras in between the sheets and we kept things very platonic.

That is until the stars came out.

Everyone had dinner, had a few drinks, and then retired to all their tents. I was sharing a tent with my friend, Todd was in a tent on his own. We had made plans for me to check out the décor in Todd's tent after everyone else had drifted off into dreamland.

Now, we all know the zippers on tents are noisy, but I tell you, my heart was beating louder than the zipper was zipping as I tried to sneak out of my tent. The excuse of 'going to the bathroom' was prepared in case I woke my tent mate, or anyone else up. I snuck across to Todd's tent, heart beating louder and breaking out in a small sweat from trying to be silent, and unzipped Todd's tent. In hindsight, we should have snuck off away from the tents, not that that would have been overly safe late at night with only the stars to light the way, but the noise of the zippers was nothing compared to the noise the floor of the tent and the little camping bed made. These things definitely were not designed with clandestine activities in mind.

I do have to admit, though, with both of us trying to be as quiet as possible by minimising our slow movements, with neither of us making a sound, it was a bout of quick, intense and totally incredible sex.

I only saw Todd a couple of times after that. The last time we met, it was for a picnic in a park. Conversation was a bit strained, it didn't flow too easily. It seemed our chakras were no longer aligned with each other. I remember I wasn't too worried about whether or not I would see him again when I left the park, which was good considering it was the last time I saw him. I did, however, develop a new interest in chakras and reiki.

Ego boosted.

Now, onto James.

A mutual friend of mine and James invited us both to a BBQ at her house. I really can't remember if I knew beforehand that it was a set up or not. But I loved being able to see my friend and I do love a good BBQ so I accepted the invitation without much curiosity. Perhaps I wasn't aware that she had also invited James to the BBQ at that time.

James was at the BBQ when I arrived and not long after the introductions had been made, we were left alone to chat while my friend sorted out something inside the house for the BBQ. Surprise, surprise, but I didn't complain. At that point, it was obvious to both James and myself that it was a set up.

James was a bit shorter than me, he had dark almost black hair, a cheeky smile and do you want to have a guess at what colour his eyes were? Yep, you guessed it, James had brown eyes. Who knew I was such a sucker for brown eyes.

As we were chatting, I quickly realised he was a bit arrogant with his nature. He had a lot to do with motorbikes and the stories he was telling me seemed to always have lots of girls around, the type of girls who could be models apparently. He did a few name drops of successful stunt bike riders that he hung around with, mentioned sponsorship deals, and special treatment he received at certain venues due to his stunt bike rider status. He also seemed keen to spend some more time with me.

This made him a good choice for an ego boost, there was no way in hell we could have a relationship. He was too self-absorbed and arrogant for my liking. He was quick to pull out his phone and show me photos of his bikes, the aforementioned models (who were all absolutely gorgeous and I'm sure they all had extra-large boob jobs too) draped over the bokes or even draped over him. There were more photos of his mates and their bikes and more photos of him on his bikes. There was a huge part of my mind wondering why he would want to spend more time with me when he hung around with big-busted models, but I just tried not to think about it too much. If anything was going to happen, it would just be me using him for sex.

We spent the next couple of weeks chatting and then when the babies were next at their dad's I went to James's house. He had a dog and a cat. He liked cats. Another reason why we would never amount to anything serious. I really don't like cats. He started telling me some things about his life and it was very clear that he was still very much hung up on his ex, but she wasn't hung up on him. He told me a lot about what had happened with the ex-girlfriend, basically everything except why they had broken up, but I did find out that she had left him.

He then told me about an injury he had received many, many years ago. According to James, this injury was to a particular part of his tackle box. His balls to be more precise. He said it was incredibly rare for him to actually cum, which meant that he could go for hours in the bedroom.

I couldn't be sure if he was telling me the truth as he explained the injury to me, if he was feeding me lines, or if he was trying to brag about his stamina, but I didn't see the issue with this. It would be good if all this effort leading up to doing the horizontal tango would be for more than 10 minutes of mediocre action. As long as he could keep going, that meant that I could keep going to, right?

The second time I hung out with James, things got exciting. We had a great evening. He'd cooked dinner and we had a couple of drinks. And wouldn't you know it, things moved into the bedroom. He was impressed with my flexibility and we kept moving around into different positions. About an hour into our horizontal fun and games, I started to feel a bit tired and sore from all the stretching, bending and banging. At one point, he kept telling me to squirt with every thrust he made. I began to think that this just wasn't worth the effort but felt bad that he obviously wasn't going to finish.

Don't get me wrong, I did enjoy it but not the way I thought I would enjoy a marathon session in bed. I decided that I should put the focus on him, mostly to give my legs a rest from my knees being pressed into the bed over my shoulders. My body was sore and shaking, my vag-jay-jay felt dry and achy. I stretched out, got comfortable, and began to focus on James and James Jnr, if you know what I mean. After a little while, he started making some very pleasurable sounds. I took this as great encouragement and kept on with my solo performance. As James had told me he would very rarely cum, I thought I'd take the time to try some different techniques.

After a while I got bored so I ramped up the efforts. Then his hands started clenching and thrashing around, the pleasurable sounds got louder and his body got tenser, he started mumbling something incoherent and not too long after this, he exploded.

This is when I found out that he had been telling me the truth about it being rare for him to finish during sex.

I looked at him feeling so very proud of myself. Mission accomplished.

Then he began to shake all over, he was breathing very fast. The fast breathing wouldn't have been too concerning normally but it didn't slow down, it just came faster. He jumped up out of the bed and paced the room for a few laps, his shaky hands running through his hair. Then he walked out to the back to his home where he had a home gym set up and began pumping weights quite quickly. I followed him and was trying my best not to laugh. He sat on the weight bench and started lifting the weights, he was breathing quite deeply and quickly, his cheeks puffing out.

What the hell? There was sweat beading across his forehead, his cheeks were flushed. Was this a serious reaction to what had just happened or as he having a lend of me? I thought guys usually rolled over and went to sleep after a big session in bed.

I soon figured out that James wasn't having a lend of me at all, this was a legitimate reaction to him actually 'finishing' in the bedroom. He couldn't string a sentence together for about thirty minutes. I felt bad as I bit my lips to try and stop smiling and laughing. Yey me! I think it's safe to say that I definitely did something right.

I have to say, that this is up there in my proud moments, but it's not something I usually share in conversation. I'm guessing when I'm in a team meeting or a work conference and the management team running the meeting asks us to share a proud moment in life, they don't really want me to jump up and tell the room that I made a guy who was convinced his tackle box was damaged and he wouldn't be able to finish completely in the horizontal dance between the sheets actually finish and the act left him unable to function normally for the better part of an hour.

I never saw him again after that. I wasn't too bothered by it though. That night had been a lot of hard work, and if I was going to hang out with someone just for fun, I would hope that there was a lot less effort needed. My body reminded me of all the extra muscle use I'd put it through that night for several days after. I felt the same as if I had done a full day boot camp, except my vag jay-jay was very tender too.

We did keep in touch though with some phone calls. James wanted to cum again, and he believed I could make him do it, again. He suggested phone sex, but considering how long it took him to finish, I knew I wouldn't really be up to the challenge. So I cheated.

How do you cheat with phone sex you ask? Turns out, as the person on the other end of the phone can't see you, they really don' know what it is you're doing. You just need to make the right sounds.

While James was on the other end of the phone playing with himself and giving me a running narrative on what he was doing, I was on the other end of the phone line doing pilates and yoga poses. Turns out, when you hold the bridge pose for over 2 minutes, your body starts to argue with you. James took my moaning and groaning as me enjoying my own touch when what I was really doing was putting my body through some torturous toning exercises.

It went on for a month or so and was a win-win. James got to cum a few times and my body was becoming quite well-toned.

I put an end to it after a while; the pilates and yoga were easier to do without the worry of keeping James entertained at the other end of the phone.

It must have left quite a lasting impression on James though, as last year, about eight or nine years after this happened, I got a message from him asking if I was available to go catch up and party with him. I don't think I even responded to his question. I just hit delete. But I still felt proud.

Ego boosted.

Luke Update! I was feeling very, very vulnerable this morning, a bit terrified that it really is over and Luke just won't want to try again. I felt frustrated and scared and just had no idea what to do. So I sent him a text. This time, instead of insisting we can make it work or telling him how shit he was to me, I told him I was missing him, that I didn't want to scare him and that it just seems silly that if we knew what went wrong and we loved each other that we wouldn't work on us. I regretted sending it immediately but he also read it straight away.

Now if I were to be giving advice to a friend in the same situation, I would be telling her to not contact him at all. If he didn't have any contact, he would either miss her like crazy or he would be going off on his merry way and moving on with his life. He would either be back or be gone and she wouldn't be in the emotional hell that she was in.

As we all know, it is easy to give advice when you're not emotionally attached to the situation.

I do know, whether I like it or not, he either has to let me know that he is happy to try and work it out or he needs to tell me he doesn't want to try again. Depending on what time of day it is and how I'm feeling depends on how I feel about that. Part of me is saying to be quiet and patient, the other part is saying that technically I am single so do what I need to do to get over Luke. But I don't want to get over Luke. I want to do what I need to do to get through this really horrible time and be back with Luke.

Problem is though, I love him. More than I ever thought I could. Each day I get through is one day closer to seeing him again. Positive thinking, we will get back together. We will get through this.

Chapter 12
The Vibrator Relationship, Going Solo

Yes, that's right, readers. I'm doing this. I have an embarrassed curiosity when it comes to the buzzing pleasure givers, but the curiosity wins out.

When I was first introduced to vibrators and sex toys, there was a weird stereotype that went with them. If you liked sex toys, you were unsavoury, you were a porn star, or you were part of the many other opinions that were uneducated and uninformed.

Things in the adult toy world have definitely changed since I was a teenager. I mean teenage girls in today's age order their own toys online and get them discreetly delivered to their homes. I didn't have the courage to buy my own toys until about seven or eight years ago.

I do think it's funny that when guys have toys, it's a bit weird, but if women have toys then it's considered sexy. Most guys seemed very interested when toys were included in the conversation.

Enough of that, let's do this. Let's chat about going solo and my relationship with the vibrator.

I wasn't sure whether or not I should do this chapter, but after asking some trusted friends, the unanimous response was 'Yes!'. One even commented that the relationship with the vibrator would be the most honest relationship in the book. I have to admit, she's probably right. The relationship between a woman and her vibrator is more often than not, the most honest relationship the woman will ever have.

This chapter will buzz, suck, tingle and hum its way through my self-education and my learnings with my relationship with my ever-growing collection of sex toys.

Now compared to the age people are becoming educated in sex toys these days, I was an exceptionally late bloomer. As you read at the beginning of my story, I was very naïve and very uneducated about sex. Oh, I knew about the birds and the bees, where babies come from and the functional aspect of sex, but I had absolutely no clue about the pleasures and the explorations of it.

My first experience with sex toys was when I was married. George introduced me to a vibrator and a dildo when he began cheating on me. As you can imagine my immediate thoughts on sex toys were, for a long time, not really positive or accurate. I felt shame, negativity and a huge shroud of secrecy around the toys. I felt dirty and like I was doing the wrong thing by using them, especially after I asked George to do something including the toys and he said no.

I'd also felt like there was some sort of expectation I wasn't living up to and that's why the toys had been introduced into our marriage.

When George had left the house, I threw the toys away. There was nothing but negativity whenever I looked at them, and I just could not bring myself to try to use them without him. I was still horrified at the thought of having these toys, and my imagination had visions of people looking at my garbage bin and just knowing that there were sex toys hidden inside.

It's quite ridiculous the lengths I went to in order to get rid of the toys without anyone knowing I had them in the first place. I mean, honestly, who knows what people have in their rubbish bins? As ridiculous as it sounds, I cut the dildo up into so many pieces that it was impossible to figure out what it was. The vibrator was a bit trickier to destroy. The toy was solid and I couldn't cut it up. I put it in a plastic bag and hammered the crap out of it, but it really didn't do any damage, just a few dents here and there. I swear this plastic vibrating penis was indestructible!

I ended up putting it in a shopping bag and surrounding it with food scraps, then wrapping that bag inside another plastic bag, and another, and then on the morning on the council kerbside rubbish collection, I listened out for the garbage truck and when it was close by, I quickly put the bag of 'rubbish' into the bin.

I was so worried and anxious about people 'knowing' what was in my bin that when the garbage truck collected my rubbish and drove away, I breathed a huge sigh of relief.

Then Kent had come home from work one day with some toys for us to use too; we weren't even living together when he went and bought a little bullet and a vibrator for us to play with. He would enjoy using the toys with me when we were knocking boots but he would get very angry if he thought I had used them without him. This anger didn't help with the shame I felt when I started using the toys on my own. When I left Kent, I left the toys behind. He could have shoved them up his own ass for all I cared.

After the way both of these assholes had bought the toys into the relationship, it was no wonder I was so reserved and shy with the toys with both George and Kent. They had both made me feel like I was the reason things needed to be spiced up. At the time, I knew no different. Now I know that toys are ok and fun and accepted and that spicing up the sexual play in a relationship with toys can be so much fun. However, it wasn't until I was happily on my own and a bit more experienced in the world of sex that I began exploring the vibrator solo relationship a bit more freely.

You've just read that my first experiences with the toys weren't really good. Well, dear readers, thank god that changed. And oh boy did my feelings about vibrators and sex toys change over time.

My cousin and I went out for dinner one night and she decided it was time to take me to an adult shop. We finished our dessert and she drove us to an area in town where there were several stores to choose from. I had never been in one before and I was excited, horrified, embarrassed and curious all at the same time. It was a very eye-opening experience as I looked at what was on offer. The costumes, the lubricants, lingerie, blow-up dolls (male and female), games, there was lots of leather and feathers. And then there was even an entire wall filled with vibrators of different shapes and sizes.

Talk about having an educational experience! Rabbit vibrators, dolphin vibrators, G-spot or clitoris vibrators, dildos, single or double-ended! There were even dildos that stuck to a surface so you could 'ride' it! There were bullet vibrators and wand vibrators, remote control vibrators and old-school plain vibrators. There were silicone, glass, textured and beaded vibrators. There were small ones the size of lipstick, there were huge ones that looked impossible for someone to be able to take in. There was a section for the women, a section for the men and a section for couples.

I embarrassingly admired a couple who were looking at some toys and discussing if they thought they'd be worth buying, anyone would thing they were talking about a new fry pan and not some huge beaded purple toy. The shop was busy! There must have been at least a dozen people in the store while I was there. I walked around the store with such curiosity and embarrassment, I was sure they all could tell it was my first time in such a shop.

I was too embarrassed to buy something and much to my cousin's dismay, we left empty-handed.

But just because I was too embarrassed to buy something then and there didn't mean that I wasn't interested.

Back at home, I jumped online and started looking up vibrators online. Every website I looked at assured discretion and plain packaging. That was good.

What type of vibrator did I want to get? What buzzing toy of pleasure did I want to try first?

I ordered a normal-ish looking one (is there such a thing?), one that didn't seem too scary and I am positive my cheeks were flushed red with embarrassment as I added a little bullet vibrator to my shopping cart and completed the order.

It seemed all I could think about over the next few days was my online shopping order that was due to arrive at any time. In a weird and crazy way, waiting for the toys to arrive was like I was initiating foreplay with myself.

Finally, the toys arrived. When the babies were at their dad's for the weekend, I went to buy some batteries—and I swear the checkout operator new exactly what I wanted the batteries for—and I went home to experiment with my new purchases. Logically, I know that no one knew what I was doing, or even cared for that matter, but I swear everyone was looking at me and knew what I was doing.

Now, all of the above might seem like normal type behaviour or it might seem like very unusual behaviour, I'll let you be the judge of that. But don't forget I had low self-esteem, next to no self-confidence, and a built-in shame in regard to sex toys. I went home and waited till it was dark, I shut all the blinds and jumped under the covers to make sure no one could possibly see me; mind you I was home alone, it was dark, there were no lights on and I was under the covers in bed. There was no way anyone was going to see me.

I guess it was due to my not-so-positive experience with sex toys that I needed to hide so I could play.

The uneducated part of me just thought you would just turn it on, the magic buzzing, twisting, turning, pulsing or vibrating would start and then you would orgasm. It took me a very long time, a really long time, to be comfortable with the idea of sex toys and learn that it was ok to play, experiment, tease myself and try different things. I learnt a lot from watching *Sex and the City* (God bless you, Samantha) and reading online articles about the art of self-pleasuring.

As I got more confident and less ashamed, I ordered some more toys. I heard about the remote control one that you could buy where the girl wore the clit and G-spot vibrator and the guy controlled the vibrations from an app on his phone. If only I had a guy who would do this with me. I learnt that you could buy waterproof ones, that you could get all sorts of different ones. My advice would be to make sure you double-check that you definitely do have the waterproof one with you before you sink into that glorious tub of hot bubbly water. The first time I went into the adult shop was really eye-opening, but it really didn't do the sex toy world any justice.

I kept these toys hidden, as you do, and if any of my friends began talking about toys, I kept quiet and listened all the while I wished I had the courage to ask questions and share my stories.

The first time I decided to go into an adult store on my own, I drove to a different town that was just over an hour away; this would mean I wouldn't run into anyone that I knew. Are you shaking your head in amused disbelief at me, dear reader? Or are you nodding your head and thinking that you do, or you would do, something similar?

When I said it took me a really long time to be comfortable with these, I meant it took a really long time, it took me years. And even now, as I'm writing my story for you, dear readers, I have never asked a man to use the toys on me since I asked George to and he said no.

A couple of men I have been with have been jealous of the toys once they found out about them, and I think it's silly. If they are jealous, then in my mind that meant they knew they could have been doing a lot better than they were in the bedroom department. Why else would they be jealous of a battery-operated toy?

I have learnt not to judge a man by his penis. Just because a man is well-equipped, does not mean he is good or thoughtful in the sack. Just because a man is under average in the under carriage, doesn't mean he isn't good in bed. It's the same with vibrators—just because it's a big size, doesn't mean it's going to be a big pleasure. It can be a bit of trial and error in finding which type of toy works best for you. I have invested in a couple of toys that were a huge letdown. I tried them several times but just didn't get any oompf from them. When I realise they are a dud when it comes to exciting my bajingo and tingling my body all over, I wrap them up in plastic bags and put them deep in the garbage bin where no one will ever see them again. Yep, I still do that.

I do have to admit, though, once I got to know my different toys and how they worked and what they did, I really enjoyed them.

There's a toy for the slow burn of orgasm, there's a toy for quick relief, and there are two toys that when used together have me curling my toes. There's the toy I quickly pull out and put in for when I just can't get to sleep. There's a toy for every mood.

One of my good friends told me about a clit toy she had discovered. She loved it so much that her boyfriend had to hide it from her because she used it too much for his liking. I got curious and ordered myself one. I am not ashamed to admit that this particular toy is my absolute favourite.

I just had a thought. I wonder how many shopping centre Santa Clauses have had mums sit on their laps and ask for a toy for Christmas? I bet that request would put the twinkly in Jolly Ol' St Nick's eyes.

Now that I know what the toys do and how they do it, I love them. If the house was ever on fire, I'd get the fur baby out then I'd be straight back in for my toys. Those things aren't cheap and I'm not sure if the insurance company will pay out on a claim to replace vibrators and clitoris stimulators.

Unlike a man, the toys never complain when you want more, more, more. The toys will go for as long as they have power. All they ever ask for is a recharge or fresh batteries. I tell you, when you put fresh batteries in them, it's like a whole new level. When the batteries are about to go flat, the vibrating weakens and weakens, and then it occurs to me to change the batteries. I replace the batteries, turn the vibrator on, place it where it's meant to go and then, 'Hello! Ahhhhh…hmmmm, oooooooohhhhhh.'

I have to admit, I do prefer the battery-operated ones. If the batteries go flat, just quickly chuck in some fresh ones and you're good to go. It is really frustrating when the toy goes flat and you need to wait an hour or so for it to recharge. Being half way to cumming and then having to wait for a recharge is a such mood killer.

I am a bit lazy, though, and as much as I enjoy the toys, you just cannot beat the real thing, especially if the real thing is good. I do enjoy being able to lay back and focus on the pleasure I'm receiving instead of making sure I keep the toy in the right spot while enjoying it at the same time. My preference would be to lay back and relax and do nothing but enjoy. The toys might take the edge off things but you just cannot beat skin on skin, touch, feel and taste. And when you're with a guy who knows what he is doing, well all I can say is congratulations! Enjoy. And oh my god, you lucky thing!

I'm now at the point where I can openly talk to my good friends about sex toys. I've even recommended a couple of them. Now that we're talking about them, and always these chats are after a glass of wine or three, I realise that more women have toys than don't have them.

Hmmm…might be time to expand on my collection and recruit some hand-free models. Excuse me, readers, while I go do some online shopping. Just a helpful tip for you, ladies: if you're doing some online shopping for sexy toys, make sure you clear your search history on google before you let your kids play with your phone.

Chapter 13
Billy…Ohhhhhh Billy.
Insert a Really Satisfied Sigh Here

Ok, readers. Top up your wine, hell grab another bottle. Make another cheese platter or grab some other nibbles. This is going to be a big chapter, if you get my drift (wink-wink nudge-nudge).

After my ego was successfully boosted by the three ego boosters, I decided it was time I stopped meeting guys and focused on myself and my babies for five or six months, maybe a bit longer. I had a bit of confidence back, I had my toys to take the edge off the sex drive and I had a bit of strength within myself; it was time to 'rebuild' me and be a better mother to my babies.

I had gotten myself into a great routine which gave me a good amount of self-care but also gave me a lot of quality time with the babies. I still worked the same hours of Monday to Thursday during normal business hours. The babies went to after-school care at the same school they went to on the days I worked and I would pick them up on my way home from work. When they first began the after-school care, I felt guilty that we weren't all at home together after school finished but it didn't take me long to realise that they loved going to the after-school care.

Some of their friends also went to the after-school care. They got given afternoon tea, they did craft activities, they had help with homework, they could play outside on the grass areas and school sports oval, and if they wanted to relax, they could curl up on a bean bag and just chill out. On a Friday, I would do all the housework and grocery shopping while the babies were at school, leaving the weekend to spend time focusing on the babies, exploring and having fun. I became quite good at finding adventures for us to get up to that had a very minimal charge, if not free.

There are some beautiful beaches about half an hour's drive away from where we lived and we spent a lot of time walking along the sand, swimming in the ocean, exploring rock pools and having picnics in the parks. Add to that going through the Maccas drive-through on the way home from said beach adventures and buying the babies a 50c soft serve ice cream cone each, and it just topped off their days. Every other weekend the babies would go and visit their dad which left me time to do whatever I wanted.

While the babies were with their dad, I would go for walks along the beaches which would last a couple of hours, I'd clean the boys' rooms, I'd relax with a book or watch a movie, I'd catch up with my friends and I would sleep in and have lazy time. It was my time for self-care. The work-life/personal life balance in this routine was really good. I was fit, toned, healthy and had a great sunny glow to my skin. Looking back now, I realised I was at peace with my life. I was mostly happy; I just got a bit lonely when I needed a bear hug cuddle and couldn't get one.

After quite a few months of this routine, I began to want for a male to just hang out with while the babies were away, but I didn't think that anyone would be keen for just a casual every second weekend catch-up. When I told my good friend this, she all but called me an idiot and said that scenario was pretty much what most single guys dream about. After re-thinking it, I realised she could be right.

I'd been thinking about joining an online dating site for several weeks, just to test the waters and see what was out there. One night when I couldn't sleep, I lay awake thinking over and over about joining a dating site. I tried the toy that usually helped me get to sleep on nights like this but it didn't work. All I could think about was the dating site.

To be honest with you, I was scared shitless to do it. What if no one wanted to chat to me? It would be a huge blow to the ego I had spent time boosting over the previous year. Was I able to handle that possible blow? No one but me would know what kind of reaction I would get from being on the dating site but still, how bad would I feel if no one liked what they saw? I would know if no one was interested. Considering what you hear when people gossip about dating sites, I was terrified that no one would drop me a message and say hi. I tried to sleep again, but sleep still wouldn't come.

In my exhausted state of not thinking things through properly, I decided to give it a go. Or maybe my tired brain did a smart thing? I'll let you be the judge.

I opened the laptop and began filling out the form to join a dating site online. I figured I'd just join one site, give it a week and see how it went. It took me longer to choose the selfies I posted than it took to complete the questionnaire on the dating site. As I submitted my details, a new worry came over me. What if I met with a real dickhead? What if I got kidnapped? Would I be found in a ditch somewhere? What if my leg showed up in one town and my hand was washed up on the beach in another? What were the rules around doing this kind of thing? What the hell had I just done?

I shut the laptop and went to sleep. Funny how I was able to get to sleep after I'd joined a site.

The next morning, I told my sister what I had done. "No one will message me," I told her.

"Wanna make a bet?" She'd replied, "You pay me $20 bucks for every message that you get sent."

I was so convinced that no one would send me a message that I agreed to her bet, telling her that I wouldn't be paying her anything. She laughed.

Within a couple of days, I asked her to cancel the bet.

"How many messages have you gotten so far?" She asked.

"Forty-odd".

She laughed at me again.

Some of the guys were a real piece of work. Some wanted the whole kit and caboodle, some were just total creeps. Some had me cringing just reading what they wrote and I quickly learnt how to block someone. One guy even began his first (and last) message by telling me exactly how we were going to meet, and how I would meet his family and had mentioned the word 'girlfriend' in the very first point of contact. I quickly found out how to block guys without feeling bad about rejecting them. Another guy straight up said that all he wanted was sex, and said he'd sort out a room at a local hotel and just meet me there. Ah, no.

He was quickly blocked. I figured I was just going to end up deleting every guy that came up on the screen. I would read the messages, then depending on how bad they were, I'd either just delete them or block them. There was really no one there that tickled my fancy.

Then there was a message from Billy.

Billy's profile told me that he was younger than me by about 6 years, he was about a foot taller than me, and he had light brown eyes. He seemed really sweet compared to the other jerks I'd read messages from, so I deleted all my other messages and just chatted to Billy.

We chatted for about a week before Billy suggested that we meet face-to-face for a drink.

I found out the safe way to meet someone that you'd met online was to be in a public place, let someone else know what you were doing, where you were going, what time you expected to be there and check in with them and let them know that you are alive and not in the process of being chopped up into little pieces in some psycho's secret hideout. Up to this point, it had never occurred to me that the guys were also worried about meeting up with someone dangerous and crazy, they just weren't as worried as we were.

Billy and I met at a local pub in the afternoon for a drink. We chatted for a few hours and it was nice. He asked if I wanted to follow him to his place and I said yes. Why not? We chatted for a while, had no more than a kiss and a cuddle, and I went home.

He kept in touch quite regularly for almost a week, then he went quiet for about a week, then he kept in touch again. When he'd keep in touch, we would meet up, but only when the babies were away. He would come to my place or I would go to his. We never went to a public place again after we had been to each other's houses. It seemed to work ok for both of us and trust me there were no complaints at all when we caught up. The kisses had moved on to the full dance between the sheets.

Billy knew exactly what to do to turn me into a huge quivering mess and he could do it over and over and over again without seeming to make any effort at all, and also without expecting much in return. If there was a gold medal for everything pleasure-related, hand it over to this guy. Hands down. No questions asked. All praise Billy!

In case it wasn't clear, I had no complaints.

I did have concerns that his neighbours would start to complain though. Billy seemed to really appreciate my vocal reaction to what he did to me. Billy liked to please, he liked to explore. While he was happy for me to do the same to him, he preferred to take charge and continue doing what he was doing until I had orgasmed, and more than once too. He didn't think one was enough, and I have to say I didn't have any problems with his need to give me multiple. One particular evening we were on his lounge, kissing and fondling, and we started to head towards the bedroom.

We didn't quite get that far, and on the floor of his dining area, he had me screaming sounds from my throat that I didn't know I could make. The louder I got, the more it encouraged him to keep going. I lost my voice that day, and it took a couple of days to come back. It also got very messy that day. I was terrified that I'd wet myself as this fluid came out of me with my screams of 'Yes, yes, yes!'. I'll never forget Billy smiling and chuckling at me as he explained to me that I had just squirted. What the actual fuck?

I'd heard about that before but I didn't know that it was a real thing that happened. I was so embarrassed to have this man, who was as close to perfection as you could get in the bedroom, explain to me about squirting.

Every woman should have an experience like the one I had with Billy. Billy made me feel such exquisite torturous pleasure that had me unashamedly screaming in ecstasy every time he put his mouth over my little love bead.

Ohhhh, Billy.

When we weren't making the most of our 'benefits', we would talk. When we're talking, we could hold a conversation ok? He was very mature for his age, more mature than me that's for sure. He had his head on straight with his finances and was on track to own his own home before the decade was out, he loved his family and was close to them but they didn't live in each other's pockets. He showed respect to people. He cleaned his own house, he cooked his own meals. He helped out his family, friends and neighbours if he was able to. We got on well, just like friends.

We were friends with benefits but I never caught up with him without having, ahem…benefits and benefits and benefits (wink, wink, sigh). I just couldn't understand why he was single. He seemed like a perfect guy to me. Re-read what I've written about Billy then consider everything I just wrote about him, why the fuck was he single? Can you answer that one for me? Mind you, I didn't want a full relationship with him but that's because I'd struggle with the age difference. Seems silly, I know. But what if he wanted babies, I already had my babies and by this time, I was closer to 40 than I was to 35.

After a couple of months of these erratic but very erotic visits, I sent him a message to ask why the contact was so hot and cold. Sometimes I would hear from him for several days in a row, then I wouldn't hear from him for a few more days. What was going on? In my mind, the hot and cold contact made for the possibility of Billy being in a relationship with someone else and he was having me on the side. Mind you, there was nothing about his nature or anything that he had said that would indicate that was really a possibility. The situation just didn't make much sense to me and I wanted to find out why.

He read the message in a completely different way to how I wrote it and I didn't hear from him again for a couple of months.

When he got in touch with me again, he apologised for not replying sooner and said he had freaked out at the message with me asking him for a relationship.

Ah, 'scuse me? I don't think I did that. Maybe it did come across that way? Hmm, I don't know. Oops. I didn't have the message still so I couldn't check it again. I'm pretty sure that I didn't ask for a relationship though, because I wasn't actually after one.

After he'd apologised (and honestly how many guys do you know that would apologise, especially when you weren't even having a huge argument?), Billy and I kept catching up in, the same kind of way as before. Hot and cold, here and there. No contact, lots of contact. He explained that the hot and cold were due to his work schedule. When he explained that to me, it made perfect sense. Der! I was being so much of a 'girl' that I hadn't been able to think logically. Just think of all those possible orgasms I missed out on.

But if anything, those catch-ups just got better and better. I can't believe the way I reacted to what he did to my body. Incredible. This guy must have been given some sort of road map to the female body 'cause he just knew exactly where to touch and how to touch it. He knew of places to give me pleasure that I hadn't even known about myself. And I read all those glossy magazines that told us about these things!

After a month or so, the kisses got more tender, the caresses got slower, and things began to get more intimate. When we were kissing and warming up to make woopie, it was more intense but had so much more feeling. I started freaking out when I realised what was happening, I was developing an attachment for Billy. I didn't want that. I can almost tell you the exact moment that the light bulb clicked in my head about this. We were in his bed, missionary position, he had my hands held in his pushed on the pillow on either side of my head, full body contact, deep, slow, passionate kissing, and he pulled back and stared intensely into my eyes as we both came at the same time.

Fuck.

Come to think of it, I think that we both noticed it and we both freaked out. Things just sort of died off again after a little while. I let it be this time and didn't contact him again. I didn't really need any complications like emotions and attachment. I can't tell you where his head was at about this, because I didn't ask him. From his reaction, I would guess that he was feeling the same as I was.

It was weird, we didn't really stay in touch but we also didn't cut ties, he found a way to be able to communicate through social media platforms but we didn't do anything about catching up. In my mind, though, we still wouldn't do anything about it as he was quite a bit younger than me. Every so often, he would comment on my social media stuff and I would comment on his. He would send a message just to say hi and see how I was doing, we'd chat for a few days then he'd go quiet again.

While I enjoyed hearing from Billy every so often, we didn't catch up again (Not at this point in my life anyway). And every time I did hear from him, I knew that the day would eventually come when I would have to cut ties with him completely. I can't explain the relationship with Billy very well. We weren't able to let each other go but we couldn't hold on to each other either. If I were ever to get into a serious relationship with someone again, it just would not be fair to that person, to Billy or to myself if Billy and I stayed in contact.

There was just something there, a pull towards each other, that I couldn't explain. We didn't cut ties completely, we just reduced the contact to once a month or so, and we never caught up apart from the odd message here and there.

Oh my god, Billy. I wish every woman had the chance to experience a Billy in their life. The things Billy did to me were just mind-blowing. Amazing. Incredible.

Chapter 14
Adam, the Virtual Romance

I'm not sure how long after Billy it was before Adam came on the scene, I do know it was within the same year.

Adam said he saw my name come up as a suggested friend on Facebook and he sent me a friend request. I recognised his name and accepted and we started chatting.

We had both gone to the same high school and had mutual school friends on our friends lists, which is how I became a suggested friend. We were in the same year at school and knew most of the same people, though we had hung out in different groups. We both had our first jobs both at school and out of school at the same local community supermarket where I had worked; we were both there for a few years after we'd left school, which was around the same time. Adam had left school just a few months before I had.

He worked in a different area of the supermarket that I had worked in and while we did see each other around the store and we knew who each other was, there wasn't a need for us to interact with each other that much.

To be honest with you, I had forgotten all about Adam until we started chatting and it was great to take the trip down memory lane with him and talk about people from school and people that we had worked with.

At the time when he connected with me on Facebook, Adam was working on the other side of the country in a remote mining camp and I guess he was a bit lonely. I was putting the babies to bed at about 8pm at this stage. We were no longer snuggling together in my bed and then me carrying them into their beds once they fell asleep, they were a lot older now and those days were gone (I have to admit here that I still cherish those days when we'd snuggle together and they'd fall asleep against me).

The bedtime routine was that they'd brush their teeth, we'd talk a little bit, maybe read a story or maybe have some music, and then they'd go to sleep on their own in their own beds. My babies were growing up.

My routine after the babies went to sleep was to do some housework. I'd pack lunches and get things ready for the next day, and then I would sit and watch TV or go to bed, depending on how tired I was.

Adam would usually finish work at about 6pm, but he was in a different time zone to me and was three hours behind me. By the time I'd finished my chores for the day, he would have finished work. As he worked in a mining camp, all he had to do when he finished work was eat, shower and sleep. Once he finished work, we would message each other.

This went on for a couple of weeks, then he asked if he could call me instead of sending me and endless amount of text messages and I said yes.

He would call me in the evening, every few days at first, and we would reminisce about high school, our teachers and our friends, about the supermarket we'd worked at and how it had changed. We also had a mutual interest in movies, music and trivial things. Before we knew it, we would have been talking for hours. I don't know how many nights I went to sleep in the early hours of the morning. I began going to work regularly with bags under my eyes and I'd be yawning by lunch time, but I was smiling all day long.

I began to look forward to his calls more and more. We began talking every day. He told me all about his ex-wife and his family and the struggles he was having with being able to see his child. He spoke to me about finding his real father over the last few years and how when he found his real dad, he wasn't well. He told me about how his mother had hidden information from him about his father's side of the family. I told him about my marriage, my babies and my ex-husband. We spoke about our work. He told me about his business and how he was sub-contracted to the mining company. We spoke about stupid stuff. We talked a lot. But it took me a long time to tell him about Kent.

To be honest with you, there are things in this story that the people closest to me don't know, and there are still things I haven't shared. I'm not sure I ever will.

One weekend when the babies were with their dad, Adam started messaging me early in the day if he had the day off work. One Saturday, he recommended a movie to me, a romantic comedy that he had seen and thought I would like. Ryan Reynolds was in it (hello! Yes please! Ryan Reynolds in a romantic comedy, say no more). I drove myself to the local Blockbuster store and found the DVD to hire. When I got back into the car, I sent Adam a photo of the DVD and drove home.

He replied to the photo message saying I didn't waste any time in finding the movie. Ah, again, Ryan Reynolds, why would I waste time? Then he asked me to give him 20 minutes before I started watching the movie. I was curious as to why but didn't ask any questions. I got myself a drink and some munchies, put the DVD in the DVD player, got comfy on the lounge with a blanket and Adam rang me to say he was ready.

"What for?" I'd asked him.

"To watch the movie with you."

"Huh?"

"I downloaded the movie," he'd said. "We can both push play at the same time and we can watch the movie together."

I was speechless. Adam was on the other side of the country. He was in a different time zone for crying out loud. It was a real heart-happy moment. We hadn't seen each other in 20 years, we were on opposite sides of the country, yet we were going to watch a movie together.

The movie was great, of course, it would be, how could it not be? Look at the main actor that was in it. Adam sent me messages throughout the movie, at times he rang and we would laugh together over what was happening on both of our TV screens. I do remember sitting there watching the movie with a massive smile on my face. It sounds simple, it may sound crazy. But knowing that he'd gone to the effort of getting the same movie and we were watching it together was the most romantic thing that had happened to me since Eddie had been on the scene. I loved it. It was an effort, but was also effortless.

Effortless effort, kind of like imperfectly perfect. It was amazing. Over the years, I have told may of my friends about what Adam had done that day, and every single one of them had 'Awwwwed' in the way women do when something is unbelievably cute or romantic.

Adam began sending me messages to wish me a good morning every day. After we finished chatting for the night, I would promptly fall asleep, but he would send me a message before he went to sleep and I would wake up to a nice message every single day. Every day was a different message. It started my day with a smile.

One day after that, I came home from work to find a package waiting for me on the doorstep. It was from Adam. I went inside to open it, he'd sent me some perfume. Apparently, he'd been shopping and he saw it, he liked it; he thought of me so he bought it for me.

I was beginning to fall for him hard and it was oh-so weird but I couldn't help it. I didn't know if he was saying everything that I wanted to hear, or if he may be lonely and I was easy to talk to. I didn't have any idea really what was going on; I didn't know if I was filling a gap in his life or if I was the only person around him who listened to him. Or perhaps he was filling a gap in my life that I didn't think I had. I had no idea what was going on but I loved it. He was paying me attention, he was making me feel important and special. I was enjoying it.

Our late-night phone calls continued and he would send me packages with little gifts to make me smile. On the eve of my birthday, he told me he wanted to keep me on the phone till it was midnight in my time zone because he wanted to be the first person to wish me happy birthday. Several times he had big bouquets of beautiful flowers delivered to me at work. One time, the delivery was one dozen long-stemmed red roses; that one got the ladies in the office talking. I'd never had anything like this happen to me before. I'd never been sent red roses before (and to this day that was the one and only time I was given a bouquet of red roses).

My workmates all wanted to know the gossip but they all seemed a bit concerned when I told them what was going on. Adam never asked me for any money and I quickly squashed their concerns that he was using me for financial gain. He was spoiling me with all the attention and gifts that he would send me. I loved our long late-night phone calls; I smiled at every message he would send me through the day. I didn't understand my workmates' concerns.

Adam and I began to make plans on how we were going to visit each other. After all, this was starting to get a bit out of hand with all the long and late-night phone calls and we hadn't seen each other since we left working at the supermarket. We decided that we needed to meet face-to-face to determine if this was truly real or if it was something else. Our night time phone calls and good morning messages had grown to text and video messages throughout the day and it seemed like we were always on our phones updating each other on things that had happened.

We agreed he would come to the eastern side of Oz to see me as he was on his own and I had the babies to consider. My phone bill had become insanely high and I needed to justify the expense. One month, my monthly phone bill was the same cost as the monthly rent. When I jokingly mentioned this to him, Adam offered to pay the bill for me. I refused. I was able to manage on my own. The gifts were one thing but having him pay my bills? No.

We had a date set and he planned to visit family that lived a couple of hours away when he was here. It was going to happen. He was going to stay at a hotel while he was here instead of staying at my place, we figured that it would be a good idea to make sure we both had space, mostly out of respect for my boys and also weren't stuck together constantly for his entire visit, just in case we didn't connect as well in real life as we had been over the phone. He booked his flights, he sent me copies of his flight itineraries and I'd promised to meet him at the airport. We were joking around about what wording I would have on the sign to greet him at the arrivals gate.

I had a countdown calendar on my phone, counting down to the big day. So did he. We were making plans on what we were going to do while he was here.

Then, a couple of weeks before he was due to come and visit, I woke up in the morning and there was no good morning message. The good morning messages had been coming so religiously and without fail every single day, some days there was more than one, so I instantly figured something wasn't right. I knew he got up early for work, he got up about the same time I left home to go to work, but in case he was still asleep, I sent him a message. If I sent a message through Facebook Messenger, then I would be able to see when he saw the message.

I opened my phone so I could send him a message. Hmm, weird, he was in my message list last night but I couldn't find him. I searched for his name but couldn't find him on messenger. I looked for his profile on Facebook, but it had disappeared. It seemed he had deactivated his Facebook and messenger accounts. He couldn't have possibly blocked me, could he?

I got the babies ready for school, I got ready for work with a heavy, sick feeling in my gut. I dropped the babies at school, I went to work and sat in the car in the carpark. My mind was a fog. What the hell was going on?

I tried calling Adam and there was no answer. Perhaps he'd gotten sick through the night? Maybe all the phone networks had gone down. Maybe something bad had happened. Maybe his phone had been stolen. Maybe he was in the hospital. I was trying to think of every possible reason to avoid the reality.

The next day, I realised what had happened—he had cut me off. He was ghosting me. For whatever reason, he had cut all contact with me. He had completely cut every possible way I had to get in touch with him. I was devastated, heartbroken. It was as though he had suddenly disappeared like he had died. There was no possible way at all I had to get in contact with him. His phone number was still connected but he wasn't answering my calls, they just went to voice mail. Text messages went unanswered. How could I have been so stupid? I had no idea what was happening, or what had been happening for the last few months, and I couldn't make any sense out of what was happening now.

I rang and left a not-so-nice message in his voice mail. My friend was so concerned and worried about how badly I was handling it that she sent him a very nasty message that ended with words implying his testicles would be in a frying pan, being sautéed and seasoned. It may have included how he would be forced to eat the cooked testicles, I can't remember exactly, but it wouldn't surprise me if that was included in the message he received. There was no reply at all.

This man who I had been having contact with almost every day for months and months had suddenly disappeared and there was nothing I could do about it. I curled up on the lounge and cried and cried and cried. I couldn't eat, I couldn't sleep, I couldn't function. I dropped a whole dress size. It was as though he had died. One day he was there, the next he was gone. There was no warning, nothing had been any different. We had spoken the night before as usual, we had talked about seeing each other, and we were both excited. Then when I woke up in the morning, he had just disappeared. He was gone.

Now, you're probably there reading this and thinking how stupid could I be? Am I an absolute complete idiot? Well, there are plenty of people who would say 'Yes, she is an idiot'. How did I let myself get that sucked in? I don't know. I do know I was feeling a bit lonely when Adam and I started chatting. He filled a big void in my life. I was enjoying myself; Adam and I had a lot of common interests and we could talk for hours without any problem. He was thoughtful, he had been spoiling me. How could I help but not enjoy it? He hadn't asked for anything in return from me apart from my time and my company. I really could not understand what had happened.

One day we were counting down to when I would pick him up from the airport and the next there was nothing; it was like he no longer existed.

I was grieving, and I was responding to him cutting me off as though a close loved one had passed away.

It took months before I heard from Adam again, I think it was close to three and a half months. His message was full of apology. He acknowledged listening to my voice mails (I may have sent several messages, some he may not have been able to understand through my hysterical tears), and also reading the message about how my friend was planning on castrating him and frying up his balls to him on a dinner plate.

He apologised for the heart ache he'd caused me, he said he hadn't intended on doing that at all. He explained that he'd panicked. He said he was considering upending his life and relocating to live near me and he just totally panicked. He'd said what if it didn't work out? What would he do if he'd changed his job, moved across the country and started all over again but for no reason? He was only meant to be coming for a visit, the flights he had booked had included a return flight. He wasn't moving here, he was visiting. I guess he was thinking more long-term about us than I had been at that time.

I understood where he was coming from, but deep down I'd thought he was a complete and total ass. He could have told me that's how he was feeling. Would I have still been upset? Probably. But at least then I would have known what was going on and not be left standing on a small patch of land, just big enough for my feet, tethering atop a tall, thin column and wobbling over a bottomless abyss while torrential rain poured from the storm clouds above my head, tears cascading from my eyes, mascara running in black rivers down my face and I thinking over and over and over, what the fuck had just happened.

We chatted on and off for a while, just lowkey chit-chat, mostly about football or politics. Crazy combination, hey? We had gone from intense, long, talk about everything conversations to polite and general chit-chat. He always deflected from answering personal questions but seemed to always ask me questions relating to whether or not I was seeing someone. Contact was very hit-and-miss, but if I forwarded him a joke or something I thought he would be interested in, he would always reply. Adam had shown me romance, he had opened my heart and I had loved him. It wasn't until he cut contact with me that I realised I was completely and totally in love with him.

Adam avoiding me hurt more than what George had done to me; I guess it could be because what Adam had done was completely out of the blue. Or maybe because everything had been so perfect it never occurred to me that Adam could hurt me. It took me a long time to get over what he had done to me. I continued to stay guarded, my protective wall around myself was getting higher than it had ever been before. I was not going to give Adam the opportunity to hurt me again.

This hit-and-miss contact continued for a few years, but when I met Luke, I put a stop to it. Sometimes there's nothing wrong with having contact continue when both parties are purely platonic, but I couldn't do that with Adam. I don't know how or why but I had allowed myself to be vulnerable with him and I had let my invisible wall of protection that I surrounded myself with crumble down. When he cut all contact with me, he had broken my heart. I unknowingly had rebuilt that wall ten times higher than it had been before Adam and I started talking. Purely because of how much I had felt towards him and how much he had hurt me, I couldn't continue a platonic friendship with Adam.

Last I heard, Adam was travelling around the country going from job to job. He still drops me a message every month or two. If I reply it's just a short, closed-ended polite response. Nothing more. Then the last time I heard from him, I didn't respond. When things began to get too comfortable or too familiar in one place, he would pack up and using his long list of contacts, he would find another job somewhere else and would go there for a while. It's his habit, it's his life. He is running from something and I don't know what it is that he is running from, I don't even think he knows what it is.

Thinking about things now I believe that Adam is hurting that bad from things in his past that he will be running from the rest of his days. I think he feels that it is easier to keep running than it is to face his past and deal with the things that have hurt him. Adam is running from past trauma, and whenever something begins to feel great, he runs. Whatever the reason is, he will never settle down. It's sad to think that Adam will never find happiness.

I had no idea what that whole situation had been exactly, but looking back now, I was grateful for it. Adam got me through a tricky time. I had helped him get through a hard time. We had been company for each other. He had built up my confidence, he made me smile for many months. He showed me that it doesn't take much effort to make a lot of effort and that it doesn't take much effort to make someone feel incredibly special. He made me believe in love again before he smashed my heart with a sledgehammer.

As I mentioned earlier, after Adam I added many more rows of bricks to my invisible wall of protection, and god help the poor sucker that had the courage to try and knock down that wall.

Chapter 15
Shane, Oscar and Josh, the Fill-Ins

Ok, the fill-ins.

Now you're probably thinking, there have been so many guys in this story so far, and you're right there have been a few. I must admit, I'd forgotten about some of these guys until I started writing out my story. It's amazing the things you remember when you start going for a trip down memory lane. Some of the memories have been really nice to remember, such as the Eddie chapter. Others have been sucky.

Now, dear readers, top up your wine or perhaps drink a bottle or two of water at this point. Though being a bit wine-tipsy would definitely make this story seem a lot more interesting than it actually is. We're going to move onto the 'fill-ins'. At these particular times of my life, I didn't think of these guys as just being fill-ins but looking back now, I can see that is exactly what they were. Poor buggers, I wonder if they had any idea that I just really wasn't that into them and I was unknowingly just using them for company.

The first fill-in was Shane.

Shane was a couple of years older than me, he was a little bit shorter. Brown hair and brown eyes (Seriously! Brown eyes again!). He was a gentle soul and seemed eager to please. We didn't really go out on many dates, we just hung out together. He had a house about 15 minutes from where I lived and on the weekends when the babies were with their dad, I would catch up with him. He had a beautiful house that he'd built, with a large backyard and a boat. He had a great job, respected his parents, had friends who were protective of him and he just didn't stop fussing over me, which was nice at first but quickly got very annoying.

Shane and I had been hanging out for a couple of weeks and there had been a few times where I had wondered why I was seeing him, but he was sweet, so I thought I'd keep giving him a chance. Everything he did seemed to focus on me.

To be honest with you, it was a bit annoying how he kept doing everything that he thought I wanted him to do, or things that he thought I'd enjoy. He completely ignored his own likes and interests and focused only on me and my interests. Don't get me wrong, it does sound nice. It really does sound nice but it is incredibly annoying.

The whole short period of time that I spent with Shane was mostly him trying to impress me or make me happy. But as I said, he was quite sweet. By this time, I had begun to wonder if I was just attracted to guys whom I felt the need to help, whom I felt I had to prove myself to, or the kind of guys who just took advantage of my good nature and would end up hurting me. I was finding it difficult to be dating a guy who was putting me first. As Shane was so sweet and thought I was pretty awesome, I tried to see past my reservations and we kept dating. His attitude towards me was different to what I had experienced before.

He met the babies as my friend and nothing more. He was great towards them and they liked him. All the while there was this voice in the back of my mind asking me what the hell I was doing. If I just wasn't that into him, why did I keep on seeing him?

Shane would always play with my butt. We would be walking somewhere and he would just start rubbing his hand over it, we'd stand in line somewhere and he'd be behind me rubbing my butt. I kept asking him to stop, that I didn't like how much he did it, and that I really didn't like it when he rubbed it in public places, especially when my babies were around. His reply was, "But I like doing it."

With his reply, it was obvious that playing with my butt was the one thing I didn't want him to do that he was going to do.

He lived alone and worked long hours, and this one day when I was at his house, his mum and dad dropped by. Holy shit, I was meeting the parents already! Shane was an only child and his parents lived close by to him. I mentioned that he respected his parents but I didn't mention that they basically lived in each other's pockets, which was one of the first things I found out when I met them. His mum would do his housework for him while he was at work and she would drop a cooked dinner into his kitchen when he worked late, ready for him to eat when he got home.

Sometimes she even had the timing perfect that the dinner plate was still warm when he walked in the front door. She helped him with his washing when he was working long hours and even got groceries for him.

This should have had the alarm bells ringing off their hooks, shouldn't it? Nope, gullible me. The alarm bells only jingled softly. I let him tell me that he let his mum do this because it gave her something to do, he didn't ask his mum to do it and she just offered so he let her. His parents were retired and it gave them a sense of worth to continue looking after him. Ok, I bought the story. The alarm bells were calmed, momentarily.

A week or so after this meeting of the parents, the babies were with their dad and I went to visit Shane at his house. Thankfully, it was just Shane and I there (his parents had taken to dropping by when they knew I was going to be there), night had fallen and he had locked up the house. We were in the kitchen when he started to kiss me; the kissing grew more heated, it was a bit more intense than it had previously been. Ok, I guess tonight was the night he wanted to go a bit further. Things heated up quite quickly. He half pushed half lifted me up onto his kitchen bench, removed my jeans and panties, and then he…ahem…had some dinner.

When Shane was finished (notice I said when 'Shane was finished'? Yes, I was not finished by a long shot. I don't think I would have been able to finish with Shane to tell you the truth), he said, "I'll think about this next time I'm at work and I know mum is cleaning my kitchen for me. Bet she doesn't know this happens on the bench as she cleans it."

Um, what the fuck? I mean what the actual fuck? Why the hell would you say that? Why in god's name would you tell the girl you'd just growled out that you'll smile next time your mum is cleaning your kitchen because she doesn't know what happens on that bench? Isn't that weird? It's just wrong. I mean, come on. Ewwww. No, no, no, no, no!

When I told Shane I didn't think we should see each other anymore, he got angry. I remember him telling me that I should consider myself lucky that he was willing to be with me, considering how I looked. What the hell? There was nothing wrong with how I looked. I was average. I wasn't fat, I wasn't thin, I was fit and healthy. Considering he had issues keeping his hands off my ass, I think that comment was extremely uncalled for.

Good riddance Shane.

I don't know what the time frame was here, it would be about a month or so if I had to guess, but I was getting bored with my own company again. I have friends, beautiful and amazing friends, but my friends all have their own lives too. Some of my friends had young children, some of my friends didn't live nearby, some of my friends were single parents and getting the chance to hang out with me every second weekend wasn't an option. I understood this and continued to seek some alternate company.

Time for Fill-in number 2. Let's chat about Oscar.

To help with my boredom, I jumped back onto online dating. One of the many guys that started chatting to me was Oscar and he seemed ok, as most of them do at first. We met for a drink at his local pub, had a good chat and a drink or two, and then I went home. I don't think I was really too into Oscar. Don't get me wrong, he was pretty handsome. Oscar was taller than me, had darkish hair and does anyone want to guess what colour his eyes were? Yep, you got it right, they were brown. His brown eyes were chocolate brown, deep and dark. He had what I would describe as chiselled features with a square jaw and an athletic frame. To be honest, Oscar was fucking gorgeous.

Over the space of several weeks, Oscar had sucked me in. He gave me the sob stories, he had me feeling sorry for him, and he had me trying to help him and fix all the injustices that had happened to him. Here we go again, my soft heart and nurturing nature would be the death of me. I really need to toughen up.

Oscar played me, I know I let him, but I really didn't expect to get played again. I really didn't think there could be so many assholes in the world, and that I would meet another one of them. I am my own worst enemy at times and I always try to give people the benefit of the doubt and try to see the best in people. Most of the time it's the worst possible thing I can do to myself. But here I was again, trying to believe that this man was telling me the truth. Maybe I let him play me so I didn't have to accept the fact that it was happening to me. Again.

If I just kept going on with things, I wouldn't need to acknowledge whatever it was inside me that kept allowing myself to get into these fucked up situations. Maybe I was using the 'ignorance is bliss' card.

Oscar was quick to tell me about his wife who he said was nuts/mentally unstable. He also had two children with his ex-wife and he told me she was brainwashing the children against him. He wasn't able to get them for overnight visits, the children didn't seem to want to spend time with him and the kids would yell at him and be disrespectful when he did get the chance to have them in his care. He wasn't working but was currently on workers' compensation and doing a payout claim through his work for a debilitating long-term injury he had received. He was employed in one of the emergency services.

He mingled with the police officers, the fire fighters and the ambulance teams and he obviously knew how to play the good cop, bad cop mind games very well. I will tell you that Oscar played the victim very well. Incredibly well. I would see him when I didn't have my babies. He obviously picked up on my soft-hearted nature and pulled every string I knew I had, and then pulled some I didn't know even existed. My friends warned me about him but I believed the stories he was telling me. I didn't believe I could get played again. I believed he was the victim.

He wined and dined me and after almost a month, he got me into bed. He wasn't really anything to rave about, but at least he would let me cum before he would finish. One thing I remember about bumping uglies with Oscar is that he would always say 'Squeeze my nipples, just squeeze my nipples'. He'd hold his head up high and thrust his chest towards me, his movements would slow down and the more I squeezed and tweaked the nipples, the more he moaned. The harder I did it, the more he loved it. I know it sounds bad but this was just weird, it was like his penis was controlled by his nipples.

I hadn't come across this before. I had no issue with doing what the man enjoyed but this just got weird. As he would consider my needs, we did sleep together quite a bit. I'm giggling a bit here as I write this. I can still picture him saying, 'Squeeze my nipples', eyes half open in ecstasy, mouth in a moaning 'O' formation.

After a couple of months of dating Oscar, I met the ex-wife. She seemed to fit the description that Oscar had given me of her well, and the kids did too. They definitely did not hold much respect for their father at all.

I was still working four days a week. While I was at work, Oscar would go to the pub and bet on the horses and he would have a beer or three, or ten. He would tell me that these things relaxed him and helped him through the stresses he was facing in his life. He never came to me drunk, he never asked me for money. Being so independent, I didn't really think too much of it. I felt that he was entitled to do what he wanted with his time, especially as he was funding his lifestyle himself.

Yes, I know. I'm an idiot. Turns out I am an idiot who is completely oblivious to the sounds of alarm bells as they ring; I only hear them after the relationship's over.

After a while, I began to notice that he really didn't seem to have any trouble socialising, but when it was time for him to be responsible or possibly talk about finding a job, he would crumble and say how hard his life was. Oscar wasn't stupid though, he would always somehow work into these conversations that I was saving him, that I was the good thing in his life. He began to tell me that he loved me and when the conversations were more serious about him doing more for himself and he knew I was getting more frustrated, he would tell me how he wanted to get better and fix his life so he could marry me. I didn't realise at the time that he was using flattery and charm to control me, and I am ashamed to say it was working; he had me believing everything he said.

It took me a while but eventually, I woke up to myself and to what Oscar was doing to me. It was harder than I thought it would be to get rid of Oscar. He kept telling me that I wasn't in the right head space to be making such decisions, that he loved me and I was keeping him together in this horrible period of his life. Uh, no. I began to fear if I did enforce a break that he may hurt himself (I didn't know then that this was a form of him controlling me). Once I began to see through his little game, I realised he was just a guy who would latch on to any unsuspecting female to let him ride his pity train and support him through the process.

Bye-bye, Oscar, feel free to lose my number.

He didn't by the way, he didn't lose my number. He contacted me about 2 years ago, just wanting to tell me that his huge work claim had come through and he'd bought himself a beautiful big house. He was bragging about his situation, then asked how I was. By this time, I had some things to brag about too and he didn't like hearing what I had to say. My work had changed and I was headed up into management, I was becoming quite successful in my career. After he bragged to me, which I am convinced was an attempt to make me feel bad about ditching him, I bragged to him. It felt great.

I haven't heard from him since.

Enter fill-in number three, Josh.

Not too long after Oscar exited my life, my neighbour asked me to pick something up from the supermarket for her when I was stopping to pick up a few things after work, which meant I needed to go to her house when I got home. My hair was a mess, I was tired, and I'd been losing weight (unintentionally mind you. Pisses me off it does. I have tried losing weight for 2 years now and nothing shifts but back then, all I had to do was be busy and the weight would fall off me.), so my work pants hung low and I walked on the hem with each step. I didn't have shoes on, I'd taken them off as soon as I got home, my work shirt hung around my frame and I was a scruffy, rushed, frazzled mess.

I walked into my elderly neighbour's house to give her what I had picked up for her (I think it was biscuits) and she introduced me to the man that was sitting at her dining table.

Josh.

Dark hair, brown eyes and a cute, cheeky smile. Yes, another pair of brown eyes. He was a bit cocky and had bucket loads of charm and charisma about him. When our eyes met, the world around him seemed to disappear. You know that whole moment in the romance movie when the screen goes blurry around the hero's face and the only thing in focus is him? Well, that's what happened. It was so weird, it was like time truly did stand still. It was a real movie moment. I do remember that he was holding a coffee cup.

I snapped out of the trance I was in and said hi, had a quick chat with my neighbour as I gave her the items I'd bought for her, and then went back to my place across the road. The boys were there and even though they were older now, I didn't want to leave them alone for more than a few minutes. I was tired. I needed to get dinner sorted for us and I looked like I'd been put through the wringer—my hair had escaped from the ponytail tie and was framing my face, my work shirt was untucked and creased, and my work pants sat over the top of my bare feet, the hem of the pants dragging on the ground.

About ten minutes after I'd gotten back to my place, Josh sent me a friend request on Facebook. Now I know I've mentioned Facebook a lot in this story so let me explain to those readers here who may be under 35, Facebook is what we 35+ people use. We use it the same way younger people use Instagram or Snapchat. It's our social media connection. It's how we cyber-stalk people. When we think we want to get to know someone, we send them a Facebook request and go through photos, and posts and just generally stalk them.

Now there are people out there who don't do this, and there are people out there who do this, and there are people out there who say they don't do this but really they do, which is the majority of us.

Josh and I began talking here and there, and soon our message conversations became day-long text message chats. After a couple of weeks, we went out on a date, I can't remember what we did though but it was nice. At the time I felt like sparks were flying and it was all so exciting. But as I write this, I realise that while it may have been exciting, there weren't really any sparks, I was just excited about getting attention again. He quickly told me about his ex and how traumatic the breakup was for him; he told me about a huge credit card debt he'd been left with because he paid for a huge fancy tropical holiday to impress her but she bailed on him. He was left to pay off his huge debt and with a broken heart and really wasn't in a good place to go into another relationship.

We began hanging out, not so much in public or with other people but at my place. He would drop in on his way home from work and meet the boys (as a friend of mine only) but everything was kept strictly platonic while they were around. We would sit and talk for hours then he would go home. When the boys were with their dad, Josh would cook me dinner, we would snuggle on the lounge and watch movies and kiss, and then he would go home. After a while, he started to stay the night, then he would go home first thing the next morning.

He would send me messages most mornings to say good morning and we would chat through the day. Not too little that made it seem obligatory, not too much that made it really time-consuming, but just enough to keep me smiling. He would send me photos of himself with little messages while he worked. Once he even sent me a bunch of bright and cheery flowers to work with a card that simply said 'Just wanting to make you smile'. I was working on the front desk when those flowers were delivered and there wasn't anyone else around in the office to show them off to. But they had made my day. After a while, I asked him why we don't go to his place, and why don't we go out and do things, but he just deflected and didn't really answer.

Every second weekend when the boys were with their dad, I would see Josh, mostly on the Friday nights at my place only, or we would meet up somewhere for brunch on the Saturday or Sunday morning. Whatever it was we did, it was just that one thing. When he stayed the night, the bedroom activities were a bit different to what I had been exposed to before. He seemed to really want me to play with his butt and I really didn't know what to do here. I spoke to a very close friend about the things Josh did in regards to his butt and she told me about rimming.

I'd never heard of this before, my friend was laughing at me as she explained it. She advised me to just give it a go because it was obvious that it was what he wanted, and she suggested a few other things I could try in this area as well.

Ah, no. No chance in hell was I going to put a finger, let alone my mouth, anywhere near that poo shooter. Uh huh. No. Nope. Nada. Not going to happen. I didn't have any issue playing with the butt cheeks but anywhere near what was enclosed in that butt crack was definitely an area I wasn't going to go near. I felt bad at first for not doing something he so obviously wanted me to do. When I had mentally decided that was definitely not going to be happening, I felt like I was a bit of a prude, maybe a bit mean for not giving him what he wanted.

I quickly realised though, that it didn't matter what it was he enjoyed; it was his choice and his right to enjoy it, but it was also my right and my choice to not do something that made me feel like dry retching and scrubbing myself clean with a kitchen scourer. To give Josh credit, he didn't complain about my decision.

He was playful and liked to have fun. There was always a smile on his face. And I noticed there always seemed to be a drink in his hand too. Josh really was hiding a lot, he was sad. Instead of pushing me away, it made me want to try harder. What a fool I was.

We came up to a long weekend and he was at a pub with his mates all day on the Sunday. He was sending me flirty and cute messages all afternoon, and when all of his mates started going home, he suggested that he could have come to my place, but as he'd been drinking he couldn't drive. Yep, you guessed it. Stupid me told him I would come and pick him up.

Now, I can feel you rolling your eyes at me, dear reader. It was very obvious that it was a booty call to everyone but me. I truly believed that he really did want to see me. As mentioned, the boys were with their dad for the long weekend so I drove off for the 30-minute drive to pick up Josh and drove the 30-minute drive to take him back to my house.

On the drive back to my place, he told me all the fun things we were going to do together the next day. I began to get excited, it sounded like Josh was going to spend the whole day with me. We were going to watch movies and go out for a meal and just have a great day together.

The next morning, we woke up and he had some messages on his phone. He apologised and told me that he'd forgotten that he had promised he would help a mate do something with his house or move house, fix something, I can't remember exactly which one it was, and asked if I'd mind just driving him back to his house.

I drove him back to his place, it was the first time I had been where he lived. I didn't go inside, just dropped him off out the front and I told him I hoped he'd enjoyed the booty call. Mind you, there was no enjoyment in my voice, I was angry. He denied it had been a booty call. Really? How could he deny it?

Josh seemed totally oblivious to how I was feeling and kept sending me messages on and off. I would respond, he would suggest catching up, I would look forward to it, he would cancel, I'd forgive him. Then he would send more messages, he would suggest we should catch up, I would look forward to it, and he would cancel. This circle happened for a little while. Then I realised that I was just a bit of fun, I was the backup plan for when he wanted some action and no one else was available. He didn't like to be alone.

Needless to say, things died off after that. I didn't deserve to be treated like that. I kept questioning myself though. What had I done wrong? What was going on? Was he just using me (uh der! This one is an obvious yes!)? I kept going over and over things in my mind, and not really just for Josh but for the other guys too. What was wrong with me? Why did I keep ending up giving my time and attention to these guys who just used me?

Almost six months later, about six weeks after I had first met Luke, Josh rang me out of the blue. He apologised for how he had treated me. I just realised that I have had three guys apologise to me for how they treated me, wow! How about instead of treating me badly, you don't be a dick, act your age and talk to me. He said that when he had met me, he still wasn't over his ex, he was struggling to sort his life out, that he wasn't happy with where he was at and it hadn't been fair to drag me into it. I listened to him pour his heart out and ask me if we could perhaps meet up again. I took great pleasure in telling him I was dating someone and that I was feeling some serious potential about the amazing guy that had found me.

Now, dear reader, can you answer this question for me? Was Josh a fill-in for me, or had I been a fill-in for him? Perhaps it was a bit of both, and I had just been a typical girl about the whole thing.

Luke Update! We had a chat yesterday, he asked me some questions and I answered them. He tried to tell me that I had hidden things from him. I'm not too sure I had. I had told him about a couple of things that had happened when they happened but he hadn't been too keen on talking about it; is that my fault for not forcing him to talk about it at the time? Had I really hidden things from him if I had tried and he didn't want to hear it? I've had time to think this evening and I started to get a little pissed off. I am realising how he is trying to put the blame on me for things that he wasn't happy with.

Well, buckle up, buttercup, I'm running out of patience. I have a little list of my own with some questions I would like to run through with him.

I did tell him I was writing my story out, and that I had learnt things about myself during the process. You, the reader, may have picked up on what I was doing wrong straight away as you have read what I have written, but it has taken me writing this all out to figure some things out, and some of the things I still didn't pick up on until I re-read this the second or third time.

Now, enough of these Luke updates. Let's just get on with the Luke chapters.

Chapter 16
Luke
Is Luke My Ever After?

Several months after I woke up to myself with Josh and had ended whatever it was that we were doing, I was out to dinner with a friend. It was a Friday night and we were at a local pub. Over dinner, I told her I was done with guys and relationships. I was over it all. The guys had all been using me, I'd been through the wringer with them all, and there seemed to be no point. I was through with being used, taken advantage of, abused and cheated on. I'd had enough of looking for the dream of a romantic partnership. I would just go out and find myself a special 'friend with benefits' type of person and stay single for the rest of my life.

I was done with relationships, and I'm hoping that after reading my story so far you, dear reader, can understand why. At this point, all I wanted was someone to scratch the itch when it needed scratching and to live a single life in between.

My friend and I argued for a little while over why I couldn't give up on relationships, and why I couldn't give up on love. She argued that I was too young, that there were some great guys out there and all that stuff. She made me promise that the next time someone asked me for my phone number, I would give it to them. As I was convinced that this would never happen, I agreed. I had met guys through friends, I had met guys online. I had met guys in other ways but never had a guy just ask me for my phone number. It was never going to happen. I would have bet any amount of money on it.

When we finished our meals, we went out to the front bar to have another drink before we headed home. There were people everywhere, it was a busy night. We managed to find a table and we sat down across from each other with our drinks and we kept on talking.

And guess who I met on this night? Yep, the one you've all been waiting for. The guy who is responsible for me writing this story of my relationships. This was the night I met Luke.

He walked by our table and recognised my friend and stopped to say hi. He had obviously had quite a few drinks, he was wearing a baseball hat and had sparkly, cheeky brown eyes and dimples when he smiled, which was a lot. I instantly thought he was very sweet, very cute. He had a nice deep voice and I just couldn't stop smiling at his smile. Those dimples sucked me straight in, as did the sparkle in his eyes.

Apparently, he thought I was a bit of ok too. In his very tipsy state, he cupped his hand around his mouth in a bad attempt to whisper to my friend, and I heard him say, "She's gorgeous!" I laughed at him and told him I could hear him.

He said he couldn't take his eyes off of me and then he said that I was probably too young for him. We figured out that I wasn't, I was only a few years younger than him. And then Luke asked me for my phone number. I'd looked at my friend thinking she'd set this up considering less than an hour before she had made me promise I would give my number to the next guy that asked for it, but she insisted she hadn't. Luke had no idea what we were talking about and grew even cuter in his confusion. Thank god I hadn't placed a bet on anyone asking for my number, I would have lost almost straight away.

He put my number into his phone and asked me if it was my real number. I put my phone on the table and told him to ring it and he did. He seemed shocked and smiled and his eyes sparkled more when my phone started ringing. "You gave me your real phone number!"

My friend said she wanted a selfie of the three of us together. Luke stood in the middle with his arms over both of our shoulders and as my friend went to take the photo, he dropped a kiss on the side of my forehead.

Our first kiss.

We chatted for a little while and had some laughs and it was really nice. My babies were at home with my wonderful neighbour from over the road and it was getting close to my curfew, so I told Luke I had to go and he said 'Ok then', and that was it. He went back to his mates and my friend and I headed to the carpark. I was really hoping I would hear from him, though I wasn't really expecting to. I had thought that the little interaction that we had was all there would be. Especially with him being a little bit intoxicated.

Then not long after I'd gotten home, Luke rang me.

"Don't forget me," he said. "You and me, we're going to go on a date, ok, cheers!"

I'd laughed, he was drunk. But it was nice. I smiled. I went to sleep that night with dreams of sparkly brown eyes and dimples.

I didn't hear from him over the rest of the weekend, though he did add me as a friend on Facebook and I'm pretty sure we both did some serious Facebook stalking. On Monday when my friend asked if I had heard from Luke, I'd told her no and I wasn't expecting to either. I figured that what had happened at the pub was all it was. To be honest with you, I was disappointed. There was just something about Luke that really drew me in.

My friend told me that Luke had contacted her the day before and asked her what the best way to contact me was. Would it be best to just call me, or should he text me first to make sure it was an ok time to call? When she told me this, my heart had melted a little, that was so sweet and thoughtful. Luke rang me that night. He'd waited three days, you know that stupid rule the guys have about waiting three days to call you because they don't want to seem too eager? Someone should tell these guys that three days in plenty of time for someone else to get our numbers too. The waiting three days thing is just stupid.

When Luke rang, we spoke on the phone for a while, and it was really easy to talk to him, he had a really nice deep voice. We had some laughs and the conversation just flowed and flowed. I couldn't stop smiling. I could hear the smile in his voice too.

We were getting close to Christmas and everyone had things on with family and friends, it was a really busy time of year, but we managed to go on a double date with my friend and someone she knew between Christmas Day and New Year's Eve.

Luke and I kept talking on the phone and there were no insecurities with me wondering where things could be going, I just knew. It felt good. We had planned to go on our first 'alone' date a week into the new year, but Luke rang me and wasn't happy with that. He bought the date forward a week so it was only going to be five days (from memory) until I saw him again. He said the original date had been too far away and too long to wait. He said he didn't want to wait almost two weeks. I thought that was a bit cute.

For New Year's Eve, I was visiting another friend. Her babies and my babies all got on like a house on fire. She and I had a couple of drinks while we were waiting for the New Year countdown and I was telling her about Luke. She grabbed my phone and sent him a message, which he instantly replied too. I apologised and explained that the message had come from my friend and not me. He was happy, he said he liked that I was telling people about him. I found out about twelve months later that Luke had been with some of his good mates on New Year's Eve and he had told them that he had met the girl he was going to marry.

I mean, he hadn't even kissed me yet—apart from the peck on the forehead on the night we met—but he was still telling his mates that he had met 'The One'.

Our first 'alone' date was great. He picked me up and we went into town to a nice, but not too nice, restaurant and had lunch. It was still so easy to talk to him, there were never any moments that were uncomfortable. It just flowed so well. And when he smiled, oh those dimples and those eyes. We'd sat at the bar within the restaurant and the conversation was easy, light-hearted and fun while we ate our meals.

After our date in town, we went back to my house and listened to music. He impressed me with his incredible knowledge of artists and songs and we had a kiss or two, or thirty. I remember telling him straight away that there would be no more than kissing that day. I was happy to kiss for as long as he wanted but that is all he was going to get. I don't know whether or not he was happy with that but he accepted it without complaint. We joked around about how many dates we needed to have before we moved things into the bedroom and decided that we needed to have six dates. The kissing was so nice. I really enjoy just kissing. We just kissed and kissed and kissed. I loved it. We were great at kissing.

Fast, slow, deep, teasing…ahhh. It was magical. It was quite obvious he would have been very happy to move it straight into the bedroom, and I knew what I was feeling against my hip was definitely not a belt buckle. I'd learnt a thing or too since my teenage years. As excited as I was to feel his, uh, interest in me, I wasn't going to change my mind.

There was a lot of perfect kissing between the first date and the sixth date. The sixth date ended up with us laughing and giggling while we were in the nude and trying to fix the bed in the dark after we had broken it. We had so much fun.

Things just continued to get better and better between us.

I will always remember the first time Luke told me he loved me. There was a group of us out at a pub, and one of our favourite local bands was playing. We were all drinking and dancing and having a great night. We were all standing around having a rest and a drink when Luke told me about a trick called

Starwpedo. It's when you put a straw into a fizzy drink, in this case, it was a premixed alcoholic drink, and you fold the straw over the opening of the bottle, then you drink the entire drink. Somehow bending the straw makes it easier to drink. When Luke told me about this, I shrugged my shoulders, said ok and I did it.

As I took the now empty bottle away from my mouth, I looked at Luke, then he smiled and said, "God, I love you." Now, Luke had quite a few beers under his belt at this time and I had a few drinks too. But being female, and newly in love, I was quickly whispering with my friends, who had seen and heard the declaration of love, and I spent the rest of the weekend floating on air. Luke loved me.

After a couple of months, I introduced him to my babies and a few weeks later, he introduced me to his baby. The kids were shy at first, but the shyness didn't last long and they soon all became good friends.

Then a couple of months later, Luke moved in with me and we were both so sure we were 'The Ones' for each other. We had spoken about getting married, about buying a house, and about our lives together for our ever after.

We found a little house to buy. I was a bit hesitant because it was too small for all of us, but Luke was telling me how we could renovate it and turn it into a beautiful house; we would turn it into our home. We instantly dreamed up grand plans for our little house so we went ahead and bought the house.

We'd been together for just over a year when Luke started working away from home to get more money quickly, but it didn't work out that way. He only got paid while he was away and when you sat down and figured out what the pay was each week you were away compared to not getting paid when you were home, the options of working at home to working away from home seemed about even. I didn't see the worth it in, especially when it started putting a strain on our relationship. A massive strain. If I told him I was missing him, or try to discuss how I didn't think the money was worth it, he would tell me that I couldn't cope with him working away.

If I managed just fine and didn't tell him that I was missing him, then he would tell me I enjoyed him being away. He admittedly told me that I was just not going to win in that situation. When I'd drop him off at the airport, he would give me a peck on the lips and he would be on his merry way. Once I dropped him off and there was a couple just in the airport drop off bay in front of us, sharing a passionate good bye kiss. I told Luke that was how we should be saying goodbye. He didn't agree.

When he came home, I would go in for a big hug and passionate kiss, he'd push me away and say he was only gone for twelve days, it was no big deal. I felt completely let down. Bye-bye, romance.

Luke was tired with the long hours and being away, our relationship was mostly through facetime and text messaging. When he was home, he'd be exhausted for the first couple of days, his body would recover from the long days he worked when he was away and then he'd be back on the road again, heading away from me. I tried to appreciate all he was doing for us, but suddenly it was almost twelve months into him doing this kind of work and we were no better off financially for him doing it. And our relationship was suffering incredibly.

I tried so hard to not feel ungrateful for what he was trying to do. I tried to be appreciative. Still it was incredibly difficult. He was only home one third of the time.

I told him about my concerns, his response was snappy. He didn't see the issue. We argued.

We were still talking about marriage, though it was always just in passing. One day, he asked me about what sort of proposal I would like. I was secretly very chuffed that he was asking, so I told him. I told him that I'd want something private with just us there. Something simple but romantic. When he asked about the ring, I told him I wouldn't like anything too over the top, just something with a nice, simple and classic diamond. I also laughed and told him that if he proposed in a way were there was a big fanfare about it, it was really public or the ring was ridiculously expensive that I would say no.

I remembered Luke telling me that about a week after he met me, he was hanging out with some of his mates and he told them that he had met the girl he was going to marry. He hadn't even kissed me yet (apart from the forehead kiss on the night I met him) but he said he just knew that I was the one for him. I wondered how long he'd been wondering about the proposal before he mentioned it to me, or if he'd just bought it up randomly. After how things had been between us, was he really considering marriage?

Quite a few months after this, Luke and I were at the dinner table with all three of our babies. I was tired, I was wearing daggy clothes, it had been a long and busy day; I believe the oversized hoodie I was wearing could have been his. My hair was a mess and I was counting the hours to bed time. We'd sat down to dinner and we took turns with telling everyone about our days. Luke went last and he pulled a wedding band out of his pocket. He proposed. The babies all looked at me eagerly and their little eyes were all shining, and they were all so proud because Luke had spoken to them all about it and they knew it was coming.

He'd even asked my babies for their permission for him to ask me. I looked into each of the babies' faces, they looked so hopeful and excited. They were proud that they had been able to keep this secret from me. Even though my heart had dropped at the lack of proposal effort, and lack of diamond, how could I say no in front of our babies?

He gave me his grandma's wedding band, which was a beautiful two-toned wedding band with an etched designed around the band, as an engagement ring and the babies all begin making wedding plans for us.

Life continued but I wasn't the excited bride. Whenever we spoke about the wedding, it was when Luke bought it up. There were many, many times when I replayed the proposal in my mind, it was nothing like what I had told him I would like. Nothing. Not to sound selfish but there wasn't even a diamond. He hadn't seem to put any thought into it at all. Or maybe he had? Maybe that was what he thought I would like because our babies were there? Still, he hadn't used any of my ideas of what I would like in a proposal.

Luke and I did a lot together, we didn't argue much but when we did have a big argument, it seemed to always end in Luke saying we were done, that we were over. The first time I remember a massive argument was when we argued about my babies. We'd gone to bed angry at each other and I had headed to work the next morning without talking to him. I came home from work that day to have my older baby tell me that Luke had packed a bag and gone to his parents' house (his parents were away). I was furious. How dare he let my baby tell me that news!

Luke was at his parents for almost a week before I got fed up with the situation. I told him to either come home or move out for good and that even though I loved him, I refused to be hanging in limbo while he sulked at his parents' house.

He came home the next day. I was so happy and relieved that he had come home that it didn't occur to me that I needed to talk to Luke about everything that had happened. We never discussed it. We just made up and moved on with our lives without talking about the argument or the fact that he had been quick to pack a bag and walk out on us.

Every time we had a really big argument, that was kind of the pattern of what would happen. He would say we were over, threaten to leave, stay in the spare room, then after a few days, he'd comment about where he was sleeping in a way that would make me feel bad. I'd tell him to come back into our bedroom and we'd make up and move on with life without discussing the problems. This happened about five times in about four years. There would be other times we would argue, they would be more like serious discussions. But these situations where I would confront him about things, or he didn't like what I would say, would end in him ending things with us.

Once I ended it. I think I just jumped in first and tried to make him feel the hurt he made me feel whenever he ended things. I stood by what I said to him, though, and Luke did make changes with his behaviours. I was just confused. My close friends who knew what was going on encouraged me to just end it and move on.

I sought counselling to help understand the mess that was in my head. The counsellor asked me if I'd seen the abuse wheel. I told her that Luke was not abusing me, that I'd been in a relationship like that once before, and I never saw that counsellor again.

Each time the relationship had been deemed 'over', things would be shit for a few more days and then we would make up, have the only good sex we seemed to have anymore and just get on with life. Whenever we would argue and I would tell him what was upsetting me, we never really discussed it after. He never verbally acknowledged what I had said but his behaviours changed. I told him how horrible it was to go out to have a meal with him and to have him sit on his phone while I sat across the table from him just watching him. He began to put his phone away. I told him how I felt like the maid and babysitter and how I needed him to make effort. He made more effort to make me feel special.

I love to look after people, so the more he did for me, the more I did for him. After a while he'd stopped doing things for me, but me being a nurturer, I didn't stop doing things for him. I told him about this but it seemed to fall on deaf ears. It wasn't until the shit really hit the fan that things would change.

We began date night once a month but had to plan it around Luke working away from home and when his baby would come to stay with us; this meant some months we didn't get date night.

Each time these arguments happened, I was adding bricks back to the wall of protection I had around built myself without realising that was what I was doing. Luke could see it but I couldn't. He could feel me pulling away a little after each argument and threat of him leaving. Even though this self-protection was a result of how his actions and words were making me feel, it seemed to him that I was the one with the issues.

In between the stressful times, things with Luke were magical. We would laugh and be silly, we would go out for incredible meals, we'd do short road trips, and we would snuggle together on the lounge and watch a lot of movies. When things weren't shit, things were great. There was a long period of time were everything seemed to be amazing. At the time I was floating blissfully on cloud nine and all was wonderful. But all the issues that we had simply put a band-aid on were still there. And as most of those issues were me not being exceptionally happy with what Luke was doing, it was only me who had the problem.

One thing that is a real bug for me is Facebook. He has always been single on Facebook. I asked him why he wouldn't be in a relationship with me on there and he said 'Its only Facebook and it shouldn't matter'. Especially with him working away from home, and with us being engaged, it really upset me, but he didn't see the problem with being single and nothing ever changed there. I had thought I was overreacting to this, but after asking several people if I was overreacting, it seems I was underreacting about this one. At the very least, he could hide it from everyone but nope. This still bugs me to this day. If it is only Facebook, then what does it matter if we were in relationship together on there? He should have been proud to tell the world we were together.

With all the stress and uncertainty I was feeling, I was stress eating and I began to put on weight. He was gaining weight too, but to me, he was just even more of a huge teddy bear. It sucks how weight gain on men and women can look so different.

We had so many good times. The good times far outweighed the bad times. Luke and I had so much fun together when he wasn't working away, which was about half of our relationship. We both had a very strong love of live music and trivia. We loved hanging out with friends, we loved to enjoy life, have lots of laughs and enjoyed good food.

We took the babies on a holiday, we went away for many weekends to catch up with friends. He did some project work in interstate and I met him there on his weekends off and we explored the cities he was working near. Some friends had a destination wedding overseas and we went to the tropical resort for a week to go to the wedding; this was without the babies and I feel very selfish when I tell you it was amazing.

We did family days out, we went on road trips, just the two of us. Luke would hear about a new restaurant and we would go try out the food. We spent time with our families. We both seemed to be able to talk to anyone and get on with everyone. My friends and family loved him, his all seemed to love me.

We would watch television together and I'd snuggle into him. Almost every time I did this, I would fall asleep on him and he would never move until I woke up. Quite often he'd fall asleep too. The good times were more than good, they were amazing.

Now, to be honest with you, things have been hard and strained on and off over the last couple of years. The arguments were getting closer together and his words have become more hurtful. Last year I told him I couldn't be with him if he continued working away, it was putting too much strain on us and there was no benefit from him doing it. When he began to work away, he was only meant to work away for one year which turned into two years, and he was talking about signing up for another twelve months which would mean he would be going into his third year. I explained to him how it just wasn't fair to all of us. He found a job which would allow him to be home every night.

We have been through so many shitty times and I've put up with some real crap I never thought I would put up with again, but here I am still fighting for us. I guess that feeling of him being 'The One' is still there for me. Yes, he would yell at me, yes his words could be very nasty. But Luke never lifted his hands to me in anger; I don't believe he has ever cheated on me. And right now, I honestly don't know where we stand or what will happen but I am still fighting for us every day.

Chapter 17
Luke and What's Going On?

You've already read that we aren't together at the moment. I'll skip through all the details and just get to the point leading up to what happened this time.

Luke took me away for a weekend which he had said was because we needed it, we needed time to ourselves. We arrived in the beautiful coastal town in the afternoon, immediately went to the pub for some drinks and to bet on the horses, then we went out to dinner. By 7pm, he was sound asleep in bed. At this point, I was wondering why did we bother? I could hear the waves crashing against the shore outside the hotel room, we were in a very beautiful location, but he was so tired. We could have just gone out for dinner at home and saved the money. There was no romance, no walking hand in hand, no snuggles as we watched the sunset over the ocean together.

Apart from the restaurant, there was nothing that was different from being at home. I watched a couple of movies by myself while Luke slept next to me and then eventually I went to sleep. We woke up in the morning, went out to breakfast and came home. With all the times we had stayed in a hotel room, we had never had the great night of hotel room sex. I had mentioned it to Luke before as I felt a bit ripped off by that but he hadn't seemed bothered by it.

A week or so after this last trip away, Luke again asked me what was going on. I had been distant from him, though he had seemed distant to me. Nothing had actually gone wrong but nothing had gone right either. I couldn't give him an answer as to why things were the way they were, I didn't know why things were strained; I couldn't pinpoint anything to talk to him about. Writing this out now, I know things were strained because nothing has ever changed. The band-aids we had placed over our issues were no longer strong enough to cover the problems.

The only kisses we shared were simply pecks on the cheeks or lips. I was craving a passionate kiss, mouths open, tongues teasing and tasting, hands caressing. I was craving kisses like the ones we had shared at the beginning of our relationship.

Once I did try to kiss him like we used to kiss and he asked me what I was doing. We used to spend ages kissing, tasting, holding each other, but no more. Sex had become an act that involved no foreplay, we could go through the whole act of sex without sharing a single kiss. And as soon as he was done, we were done, no matter where I was up to. I missed the romance, the intimacy, the affection. I had mentioned this to him a couple of times before but it didn't bother him, so he didn't see it as an issue.

I'd even asked him if we could try new things and spice up the sex life, he just laughed at me. I still don't know if he laughed because he was nervous, unsure, insecure, worried, or just didn't see what the problem was.

I told him I loved him and he said he loved me. But as I couldn't answer the questions he was asking me in a way that satisfied him, he said he was calling the end of the relationship, he was leaving.

Again.

Then things got nasty. At the time I didn't know where it was coming from but now I realise it was because he was hoping I would beg him to stay and I didn't. I was used to hearing him tell me that he was leaving me and I guess I just didn't believe that he would go. And why would I beg him to stay if he'd told me that he wanted to leave?

When we would argue, he would call me by his ex's name. Now, you're probably sitting there shaking your head at him, everyone knows you just don't do that. It's just wrong. It's just asking for trouble. When we'd argue and he'd call me by his ex's name, I would usually get cranky. I would tell him it's a stupid thing to do. During this breakup, he called me by his ex's name and this time I saw red and yelled at him. But then, a couple of days after this, we were talking, we weren't yelling, just talking, and he let the beginning of her name slip out again.

Now, I do my best to not cry in front of guys. George seemed to get off on making me cry; if I cried in front of Kent, it would just fuel his rage. Once I cried in front of Luke when we were arguing and he told me I was crying because of my own actions and had no one to blame but myself. So I tried my best to make sure I didn't cry in front of guys. But this day, as he was packing his things to go away for work and started to call me by her name, I burst into tears and I just cried and cried and cried. It all started to come out.

I told Luke that it really wasn't a smart thing at all to use the ex's name, and through my tears I asked him why he did it. He wasn't saying her name accidentally, he was doing it purposefully. He said it was because he knew it would hurt me. And even though I disliked him intensely at that time, I also loved him with all of my breaking heart. I let him hold me while I cried. He stood there, wrapped his strong arms around me and pulled me into his chest, he rested his chin atop my head, and I stood there within the warm of his teddy bear hug and I cried, and cried, and cried.

He occasionally kissed the top of my head and he just held me. As tears flowed from my eyes faster than floodwaters breaking a dam wall, I realised that he loved me. It was such a horrible moment but just so beautiful at the same time. I'm not a small person by any means but Luke is a good head taller than me; he is broad shouldered, he is muscular and strong. Stepping into one of his hugs is like stepping into the safest place in the world, and I felt incredibly safe but broken while I stood there engulfed in his arms.

God, I miss his hugs. Over the last few months, those hugs had gotten less and less.

To be honest with you, I had absolutely no idea what was going on.

A marching band being led by rainbow coloured unicorns flying upside down and farting rainbows could have walked through my house at that time and I wouldn't have thought it to be weird. I really had no idea what was happening.

I really wasn't expecting Luke to tell me that only a few days after that conversation of how he was leaving, he'd found a place and would be moving out the following week. I had just assumed it would be like all the other times and he would just come back into the bedroom and we would put a band-aid on it and life would be ok again.

Luke's work had a six-month project where he would need to be away from home some nights, and he asked his boss to send him up there until it was time for him to get the keys for his rental property the following week. And that was it. He would only be back here to get his things. He grabbed his work gear and a suitcase and he left. His parting words were something about how I had finally gotten what I wanted and he was gone.

I can't remember how I got through that week. It was all a blur to me.

I remember Luke came home from work and started packing up his things. I helped him. I helped him drive his things to his new place, which wasn't too far away. What the hell was I doing?

After he'd moved out, he had to go away for work again and some furniture was getting delivered to his new place. He left me his key and asked if I would let the delivery guy in; I said yes. And I did. I have no idea why. This whole situation was just weird.

I had written him a letter, I guess I had a little vent in the letter, and I left it on his bench after the delivery guy had left. I locked his spare keys inside his house so I couldn't go back there and retrieve the letter when I chickened out and decided he shouldn't read i-which happened to be he exact the front door locked. I wasn't expecting him to mention the letter when he got home, but he did and we began to chat. This chat was us beginning to talk through things that we were concerned about. He went first. He asked me some questions and I answered them honestly. I told him we could discuss my concerns next time we had a chat like this.

He suggested that I stay at his place that night and I did. It was so beautiful. He held me, we held each other all night. I didn't sleep much, I was enjoying being with him. I was listening to him breath in his sleep and it was soothing, I'd missed it. In the morning before he went to work, he kissed me tenderly, he told me he loved me and that he would talk to me after he finished work. He hadn't kissed me like that, or held me so lovingly for a long time, over six months I would guess.

But he didn't call me after he finished work. I hadn't heard from him so I sent him a text. He wrote back telling me he felt he needed space. I said ok and told him I loved him.

Was I a fool for agreeing? Who knows. Did I believe him? Yes. Am I an idiot? Probably. Have I fallen into a sick and twisted mind game, or is he feeling the same way I am? Is he vulnerable and scared? I wish I knew the answers. He was hot and cold. I had no idea which way was up. I needed to check my phone to figure out what day it was and I was getting through the work day by running on autopilot. At times I questioned myself as to why I was allowing him to have this control over my mind. Why was I fighting so hard for something that was so damaged? Why couldn't I just accept it was over?

That night, I was sitting with my babies, we were having dinner when he sent me a text message saying there was no hope and we were done. He had completely broken up with me and he had done it via text. I immediately tried calling him but he refused to answer. I tried again. He rejected my call on the second ring. He sent a text message saying there was no point in talking, it was done. We were over.

I was a mess. My beautiful babies held me while I cried. How the hell did I end up here? Once again, I was standing on a small piece of land that's just big enough for my feet to fit on. I felt like that land is tethering atop a really tall and thin column of crumbling and rocky earth, I was wobbling over a bottomless abyss while torrential rain pours from the storm clouds above my head, tears cascade from my eyes, mascara ran in black rivers down my face and all I could think was 'What the fuck has just happened?'.

Through my work we have access to an Employee Assistance Program, which means I could register for free confidential counselling. I gave them a call. I figured I'd go on a waitlist and my situation wasn't that bad, but the lovely lady I spoke to when registering had a counsellor call me back within hours. Mentally and emotionally, I was a lot worse than I realised.

As you have read, I have been in shitty relationships before. I have been cheated on, I have been abused emotionally, mentally, socially, physically and financially. I've been played, I've been used, I've been taken advantage of. I have definitely been through the ringer.

My friends were incredibly worried about me. I wish I could put it into words to get them to understand, I know Luke had been a dick and I know I deserved so much better than what I was getting, but Luke was different to the other assholes. Luke isn't doing what he is doing because he is an ass (even though my favourite word for him at the moment is asshole). Like all of us, Luke has past trauma that he refuses to acknowledge. I understand why he does what he does; that doesn't make it acceptable, but I do understand.

God help me, most of me still believes, after all the hurtful things he has said and done, that we will get back together after a couple of months and after a bit or work, everything will be amazing. Only time will tell me that.

It doesn't help to make the heart to feel any better though. I haven't contacted him today. I have cried most of the day. My dinner tonight consisted of premixed alcoholic drinks. My babies took away for dinner. Just to put your mind at rest here, my babies are almost grown-ups. They both have their drivers licences and their own cars. I took the fur baby for some walks today but spent the rest of the day on the lounge wrapped in a blanket and staring at the TV screen, until I picked up my laptop and tried to at least pretend to work. I have stalked him online several times. I had begun to lose all that extra weight I had put on.

When my friends are in hard situations, my standard advice it to tell them to ignore their mind, ignore their heart and listen to their gut. Right now, my gut is telling me that this is different from other breakups. This is him punishing me for calling him on his actions and asking him to be accountable. When he feels he has punished me enough, he will contact me and see how I react.

Is this behaviour toxic? Absolutely. Do I deserve better? Most definitely. Will I take him back if this is what happens? At this point in time, I say yes, I will.

I've been having weekly counselling sessions, which really help. I have no idea what the counsellor is doing but it is helping. I received some good advice from her today. I was told that I need to think about what I am willing to accept in a relationship and to put down those boundaries. If the other person had behaved in a way that others (i.e., friends/family) don't like that is not something I should consider. I need to think about my feelings, what I want, what compromise I am willing to make, what I will put up with and what I won't put up with.

The counsellor opened my mind to how Luke and I both have different love languages. She helped me see that things he has been doing are his way of saying he loves me. She tried to explain to me that even if he does love me, I don't have to accept being treated in a way that is vastly less than I should be treated.

The sad thing is, dear readers, as you may have noticed that I believe that from my previous relationships, out of all the guys I have been in a physical relationship with in my adult life, Luke has treated me the best.

Chapter 18
Where Am I Now?

If you are still reading this, and learning all about my vulnerabilities, my weaknesses, my romantic life's story, then I feel like I can call you my friend. In true friendships, one friend can lovingly and openly tell the other friend that they are just being a fucking idiot and need to wake up to themselves. I feel like this is what you will be saying to me very soon. I feel like while you are reading the next chapter, you will say, either under your breath or in your mind, 'Annelia, you are a fucking idiot'. And here's why.

Just as I was reaching the point where I began to feel stronger and ready to move on, Luke and I reconciled.

He stayed in his own place and while we were living separately, the sex was amazing. There was a lot of kisses, amazing, passionate, wonderful kisses. I was so hopeful the romance had come back. I even ignored the fact that he was still single on Facebook, as you already know; he had always been single.

A few months after the reconciliation, he moved back in with me and everything was happy and amazing for a couple of months. Then it all turned shit again. No more kisses, no more exciting sex. He'd sit on the lounge and do nothing except work, eat, sleep and watch as much sport as humanly possible. It only took a month or two before I realised I'd made a huge mistake. What the hell had I done? Once again I was standing on a small piece of land that's just big enough for my feet to fit on. I felt like that land is tethering atop a really tall and thin column of crumbling and rocky earth. I was wobbling over a bottomless abyss while torrential rain pours from the storm clouds above my head.

What the fuck had I done? Why had I fought so hard to be right back where I had been before? What is it about me that makes him think it is acceptable to do what he is doing, which was not much at all.

I became bitter in regards to romance, I stopped reading romance books and watching romance movies—which I usually loved—and focused on reading a book about empowerment and strong women. I threw my all into my work. I was desensitising myself to romance. As you remember from my Eddie and Adam chapters, I really do love romance. The more Luke slid back into his old ways, the more I began keeping busy with the babies, housework and my job, and the less I tried to put romance into the relationship. There are two people in the relationship, it should not have been up to me to bring the romance or mostly initiate intimacy.

One of Luke's childhood friends found true love, and every time we saw Luke's mate and his mate's lady love, Luke would tease him about how weird it was to see him with a woman and Luke would laugh. Actually, come to think of it. I don't think I have heard Luke tell his mate that he is happy for him. Hmpf. What does that tell you?

Luke and I were having a monthly date night. All our date nights were us going to a restaurant, having a couple of drinks and a wonderful meal, then we'd go home, and he'd be asleep before too long. He would always tell me how much dinner cost, there was no hand-holding, no public displays of affection, no good night kiss, and no romp between the sheets. Don't get me wrong, the food was always amazing, but to me it wasn't a date. The part that would have made it a date was the intimacy and affection that would happen when we got home but that never happened.

I felt selfish and high maintenance by complaining about it. I was getting more hugs from my female friends than I was from Luke. I think my complaining hurt his ego or feelings, and I could understand how that could happen, so I tried to be more grateful. But he didn't put more effort into the dates.

I began having monthly dates with my babies. Luke had once complained I didn't do enough with my friends, so I began to do more with my friends. I joined a local community group. I began spending more time playing on my phone. I stared spending more time at the gym. I started learning another language. I needed to keep busy to keep myself from realising I'd put myself back into a huge mess. And to make things worse, I still loved him. The internal battle I was fighting was incredible. I was weak. I needed to be strong and speak up in a way he would understand, but I guess I didn't because I knew from experience how easily he would end things.

As I couldn't speak up, I just kept plugging along. There were times when things were great, there were times when things really sucked. There were days when I was happy he was away for work and then there were days when I was happy that he was home. It was a roller coaster of emotions that had me running around like crazy and getting nowhere.

To me, Luke and I were living separate lives, I felt like I was just making his life easy for him. I was helping with his daughter, I was looking after him, I was running the house.

We lasted another twelve months before the shit hit the fan again.

To Luke, everything had been just peachy, and of course it was. What guy wouldn't love being in a situation where someone was taking care of everything and doing everything for them? I was an idiot. I was an idiot that was the cleaner, the cook, the personal shopper, the babysitter, the companion, and the quick roll in the hay when he felt like it.

Once again, Luke started picking arguments. Once again, it was all me, all my fault. According to him, it was anyway. As usual, he tried to get the upper hand in the argument and said he would be better off on his own, that he should start looking for his own place and he would move out.

This time, I didn't defend myself, I didn't do the things I knew would make him happy and get him to change his mind. I didn't take the blame, I didn't change things to make him happy.

I was silent. I'd been in this place with him too many times already. It wasn't fair for him to keep breaking up with me every time we had a huge argument. I was done.

After a while of silence, he asked me what I wanted to do, so I threw it back at him. "You just told me you would be better off on your own."

"Well, I would," he'd replied.

"There's your answer then. Let me know when you're leaving. I'll help you pack."

He was furious. To be honest with you, I really couldn't care if he was angry, I was hurting too and he didn't seem worried about me.

The argument continued and during it, I had started to defend myself against something Luke said I had done, which I hadn't done. That is one of my pet hates—being told I did something, or being blamed for doing something which I had not done and he knows how much I hate it. Something happened to me mid-sentence of his making this false accusation. I just didn't want to do it anymore. I raised my hands into the air and said, "Nope. I'm not doing this. I don't want to be in this relationship anymore," and I walked away.

Do I still love him? Yes. Do I want to try again with him? No.

He is still in our home, he hasn't moved out yet, though he is telling me that he is looking at rental properties. Most of the time the mood around the house is quite tense. I've taken to leaving the housework and other things that have to be done for when he is home so I can keep busy, and when he isn't home, I rest and do my best to relax.

I really can't tell if he is playing mind games with me or not. A huge part of me wonders if he is struggling as I am, just as I have wondered before. But now there is a small part of me that believes he is trying to manipulate the situation while displaying authority and control. The fact that twice over the last month he just hasn't come home at night makes me think he is just being a total ass.

Last time when we had broken up and he moved out, I fought so hard for us to get back together that it scared him. This time, I'm not fighting at all, and that is scaring him too. Maybe he should just be open and honest with me, but I guess that scares him too. He needs to stop playing games with me. Maybe I do need to try to get him to listen to me again, I just don't know. I really don't know what the best thing to do is, and when I'm unsure about what to do, I don't do anything.

Every time he makes a snide comment, every time he leaves the house without saying a word to me, every time he acts like a spoilt brat or tells me he is going to inspect another rental, I just simply don't react. Apart from slamming the front door louder, he seems to not know what to do; he seems rattled that I am not doing all the things I have done before. But as I warned him last time this happened, every time he threatens to leave and blames me for everything my wall of protection I have built around myself grows. And last time I told him that if we ever get in that place again, there would be no going back for me. I told him last time we got to this point in our relationship that was the last time I would give us another chance.

In my mind, when Luke told me he was done, that he was better off on his own and that he was leaving, I was done. We were done. There was no going back.

The hard thing now is getting both Luke and myself to believe it.

It's now been two months since that fight that ended us. Two months of still living in the same house. Luke hasn't wanted to tell his baby what's going on until he finds a place to move to. We still have his baby every second week for a week and she is here with us at the moment. Luke went to play golf with mates yesterday and he was meant to be home for dinner but didn't come home till daybreak this morning. This is the third time he has done it to me, but this time pissed me off even more because he did it to his baby too.

He can't see an issue with it though. Before I would have let him tell me it was nothing to worry about and I would have just gotten over it and moved on, but now I'm not. I am allowed to be angry, furious, irate, upset and emotional. And if he doesn't like that, then he can just camp on someone's lounge until he finds a place.

Next time he's away for work, I won't be responding to any of his texts. Let him stew and wonder. He will soon learn how it feels to be ignored. Those nights he didn't come home, I was calling him and messaging him, only to be ignored. To be honest with you, though, as much as I want to be able to ignore him, I won't be able to. Maybe the issue really is me, maybe I have caused these problems. I'm a mess.

He tells me I need to stop making plans for his baby, and I need to back off and stop interfering in things. Yet I'm good enough for him to leave his baby with me while he stays out all night.

He is in for a shock. This last asshole move that he has pulled with not coming home was the final nail in the coffin. Sure, he'd had a few drinks and couldn't drive. Normally I would buy that excuse. I'm a bit proud of how quickly I thought of this response, though, if you knew you were driving you shouldn't have drunk alcohol. Simple. Coming home to his baby should have held more power than drinking a few beers. You just do not do those asshole moves to your kids.

I'm not going to be his doormat anymore.

Earlier on, I told you how I knew why my relationship hadn't been working, and that was due to our poor communication. Well, this time the relationship just wasn't working because Luke had become an asshole.

I will apologise to you here, dear readers. I'm wondering if you've become confused reading my fluctuating emotions and thoughts. It's difficult to try to write it clearly, as my mind is very confused too, my emotions are on the longest roller coaster ride in history. And what makes it all worse is that I love him.

Chapter 19
Luke is Gone, Again

Ok, dear readers. This chapter will either have you feeling incredibly empathetic towards me or throwing the book down in frustration. Either way, it might be time to top up that wine, or perhaps it's time to grab a drink of water. I guess that depends on how engrossed you have been in my story.

As you read in the previous chapter, things haven't been going overly well between myself and Luke. To be completely honest with you, I have no idea why things were that way. I've been confused and just battling to get through each day without any added stress.

The couple of people close to me who I confided in were telling me that it sounded like a toxic, abusive situation. And even though I agreed it was toxic, I was defensive about it being abusive. Whatever it was that was happening with myself and Luke was definitely not healthy but it wasn't abusive. I know Luke in a way that I believe no one else does, I get to see the real Luke, the vulnerable Luke. I see the true colours that he hides under many layers of protection. I told you about the wall of protection I have around myself, well I believe that Luke's wall of protection is even bigger and thicker than mine is.

The last big argument that I wrote about in the last chapter was now several months ago, which as usual ended in Luke saying he was leaving and began looking for a place to move to, things just never got better. The kisses have all stopped, there are no hello, goodbye or 'just cause we could' kisses anymore. Conversation was mostly strained. There were no hugs. Unless we snuggled together while we slept, there was no touching.

The fact that we would snuggle into each other while we slept did give me some hope that things might get better, but they didn't.

Luke told me he was still looking for a place to move to and there was no point staying as I wasn't fighting for us. I told him when I tried to talk about things he'd cut me off and wouldn't listen.

He denied it and said he didn't want to talk about it. He did exactly what I was trying to explain to him that he did, but he did it again while denying it.

Even though I love him, I can't keep tiptoeing around and banging my head against a wall trying to get him to understand or listen. I couldn't be the only one that was fighting for the relationship.

He was right, I wasn't fighting for us anymore. But neither was he.

Last week, he told me he had found a place to move to. He was picking the keys up on the weekend and he would be gone. Over the weekend, he moved out.

I really don't know how I feel. I'm aware that it needed to happen, but due to the history of our relationship, I am really expecting him to come back in a few months' time. And if he does, I have no idea what I will do.

The odd thing is, he has rung me twice today, yet when we were living together, we could go a week without sending each other a text or a message. It was definitely strained while he was here.

I've asked myself a thousand questions over the past few days. At first, when he told me he was going, I didn't really believe he would. Then when he picked up his new keys and began moving, the questions started.

Why wasn't I enough? Why wasn't I good enough? Was it because I'd gained weight? Was I doing too well at work? Why didn't he love me anymore? Why is he kissing me again now that he has moved out? Why are the kisses more tender and loving than they have been since he moved back in last time? Why is the passion always there when we break up? Why is the sex better when we break up? Why is he more considerate of me when we break up than he is when we are together? Why? Why? Why?

I wonder if he is feeling relieved to be free of me. But if he was feeling that way, then why was he texting me and calling me? Why is he helping me sort of things? If he isn't relieved, then is he feeling guilty about something? Or is he being nice because he wants me to fight for us? Or is he regretting his decision? Or does he still love me? Or is his mind just as fucked up and confused as mine is?

Why do we put ourselves through all these questions when things end? I've been told I'm behaving 'normal' for the situation, but that doesn't make me feel any better.

Last time he moved out, I was a mess, I couldn't function. I've had my moments this time but I've been better than last time. Am I becoming immune to him leaving because he always came back? What will I do if he doesn't come back this time? What has he been telling people? Should I tell him I still love him? Have I done the right thing? Should I have fought for us?

God, I would really love a crystal ball right about now.

Right now, I just don't understand anything. Ironically, I'm in the same position now as I was when I began writing this story. I'm standing on a small piece of land that's just big enough for my feet to fit on. I feel like that land is tethering atop a really tall and thin column of crumbling and rocky earth. I'm wobbling over a bottomless abyss while torrential rain pours from the storm clouds that appear only directly above my head, tears cascade from my eyes, mascara runs in black rivers down my face, and I just can't help but think 'What the fuck has just happened?'.

As you may have noticed throughout my story, I'm always trying to give people the benefit of the doubt. In between crying, being angry, questioning everything about my life at the moment and just staring into space thinking 'What the fuck?', I have been trying to figure out what's going on inside Luke's head. Everyone reading this will know how stupid that is but it's something most of us do. Trying to understand him is when I begin to miss him more.

People have past traumas, people have demons in their lives, skeletons in their closets. However you want to phrase it, we all have things that trigger us, that upset us, that remind us of past issues. Everyone has these things, god knows I have them. But the fact that we went through something bad earlier in our lives does not give us the right to mistreat people. And I don't believe that Luke has done all these things that upset me on purpose. I don't believe it was intentional; I never have, and I guess that's why I became stuck and partly why I avoided having those confrontational conversations with him.

In one of the Luke chapters, I wrote how Luke had treated me the best out of all the guys I'd been in relationships with. Looking back now, and seeing the way he treated me without those rose cd glasses on, I realise that he was just as bad as those other guys.

He had me walking on eggshells, he had me changing things I loved doing because he didn't really like them. When we argued, he was nasty. He never raised a hand to me but his words cut wounds I had no idea how to heal. I had been too focused on defending myself against things I was accused of that I just hadn't done, and proving my worth to him, to argue back and tell him what he had been doing.

I had gotten to the point where I loved him working away from home. I would have great days when he was away, which was a huge contrast to when he used to work away from home earlier in our relationship. I also noticed I was sleeping so much better when he was away.

When he was working locally and was coming home every evening, I would love the mornings and start to feel down in the afternoons, then once he got home, I felt some weird sense of comfort. I didn't understand why, and then one day I had the light bulb moment. You know when you say 'Ah ha!' to yourself and then suddenly, the whole thing makes sense to you? I had that moment.

I am wondering if you have it figured out already. It took me a long time to understand it, but gaining that understanding helped me get to the point of just not caring anymore. That is quite sad really, especially when I think about the life we had built; actually, I'd be more correct in saying the life that I had built that he participated in for reasons that suited him.

Back to my lightbulb moment. Well, I realised that the reason I slept better without him was because I was more relaxed. The reason I was happier when he was working away was because I was on my own with the babies and the feel around the house was less tense.

The reason I loved mornings when he was working locally and home every night was because he'd leave the house before I got up. And the reason I started to feel down in the afternoons was I knew he was coming home soon and had no idea if he was going to be in a good mood or a bad mood until he walked through the door. When everything was fine between Luke and me, I didn't have these rollercoastering emotions. But when the shit hit the fan, these emotions all road the biggest rollercoaster in the world inside my stomach.

And the weird sense of comfort, well that was interesting to understand. The reason I felt that weird sense of comfort when he came home was because I knew. I knew what mood he was in, I knew what I was up against for the evening. I knew. I wasn't wondering or guessing anymore, I knew.

As I mentioned before, Luke never laid a hand on me. I never felt scared or threatened for my safety. But I have realised that all these feelings I was experiencing were not healthy. The situation was worse than I thought. As far as Luke was concerned, I was overreacting.

He was quite good at downing my feelings. Regardless of the reason why I was feeling the way I was, he would always say, 'Don't cry about it,' or, 'No point getting angry,' or something else that would instantly dismiss my reaction to a situation. Unless I was laughing. He never told me to not feel the laughter.

So, where am I now?

Well, today is different to yesterday, which is different to the day before. Today, I am not standing on a small piece of land that's just big enough for my feet to fit on, feeling like that land is tethering atop a really tall and thin column of crumbling and rocky earth, with me wobbling over a bottomless abyss while torrential rain pours from the storm clouds that appear only directly above my head, tears cascading from my eyes, mascara runs in black rivers down my face, thinking 'What the fuck has just happened?'.

You may have noticed that I'm not as angry with him in this chapter as I was in the last one.

Now, I am feeling a bit sad. The relationship is over. There is no going back. The last time I was expecting him home and he didn't come home, I was wondering if he was in a hotel somewhere with someone. And I didn't care. I actually thought it would be good if he did and I found out about it because then I would have grounds to kick his ass to the kerb. During the wee hours of the morning, I had lain awake in bed comparing the differences to this break up to the last. Last time we broke up, you may remember reading that I was terrified Luke would meet some younger, gorgeous and stunning model material woman and forget all about me. Well, this time, I wasn't worried. If he did meet someone else, it might get him out of the house quicker.

Last time I refused to use his side of the wardrobe, I left the clothing rail bare, just waiting for him to come back and hang his clothes there again. This time, I have already bought myself some new clothes and coat hangers. The day he moves out, the clothing rail will be filled with my clothes.

Living in the same house while we are separated is hard. Emotionally it is, at times, a huge mind fuck. We broke up months ago. The hardest part for me has been the lack of change in us.

The only differences between now and when things were happy are now there are no 'I love yous' said, there are no kisses on the lips when leaving for work or getting home, and there is no affection or cuddles. That is the only difference. I do love him, but I am not in love with him. And there has been no passion for a while. The passion seemed to disappear from the relationship once we moved in together and he got comfortable. I never questioned it at first but I do remember bringing it up once. The response I got was 'Sex isn't everything.'

And it's not everything in a relationship but it sure is fun and helps keep the relationship going.

I have a feeling that after the wounds of separation heal, Luke and I will be friends. Not seeing each other every other day type friends, but stay in touch and have a chat every now and then type friends. How will I be when I see him with another woman? I have no doubt it will hurt but I think I will easily accept it. It's funny you know, I had thought that the end of a 6-year relationship would leave more of a hole in my life. Perhaps it will when he actually moves out? I don't know. If Luke keeps performing these asshole moves that he has been doing, I am pretty sure the first night he moves out I will be hitting the town with my friends and celebrating with cocktails and dancing.

And right now, right at this very moment, I'm wondering if he has finished his unpacking. Is he missing me? Will he reach for me in his sleep tonight as he sleeps in his own place? Will he call me tomorrow, or send me a message? Is he thinking about me at all?

It hurts, it all does. Geez, I really, really wish I had that crystal ball.

Chapter 20
Lessons Learnt from Looking Back

Now, in writing this story for you all to read, I have learnt a few things about myself. I am soft-hearted, I give too much, I trust too easily; I see the best in people whether it's visible or not and I give people way too many chances and opportunities to hurt me. I refuse to change how I am, but I think I might need to get some boundaries happening. I also need to make sure I have the courage to speak up when someone starts to cross those boundaries. I will need to remember that if that person, whoever they may be, gets angry at me for enforcing those boundaries then they don't deserve a place in my life.

With being so soft, trying to avoid confrontation and always just trying to keep the peace, I have contributed a lot more than I thought I had to the issues that I have experienced in relationships. I have made everything worse, and in a way, I have enabled these guys to treat me the way that they did. That was difficult to learn and understand. Keeping the peace is not always a good thing.

Knowing all this doesn't help me at the moment though.

I was 15 when I met George, the first guy I wrote about in this book. I am now 46 years old. It seems that for most of those 30 years, I've been constantly trying to do things that will keep the men I've been involved with happy. As long as they were happy, it seemed as though I was happy. The key word there is 'seemed'.

I have learnt that what I always did was make sure that the man I was with was happy. I would create an environment that allowed him to do as he pleased while I felt the need to justify what I wanted to do.

I was a people pleaser. More accurately, I was a partner pleaser.

I had thought that was what relationships were, both partners would do things to make the other happy. I was doing it without realising that my partner really wasn't doing it back.

While some of these guys didn't want that justification from me, they became used to it and when I started feeling resentful in the relationship, I would stop offering the justification. Then the shit would hit the fan. Don't get me wrong, I am not, by any means, making excuses for these guys, no way! I know each of these guys had their faults, just as we all do. Some of these guys had worse faults than others, but that's who they were. As I always say, it takes all kinds to make this world of ours go round.

I wonder how much would be different if I had allowed the difficult situations to take place instead of avoiding them.

Before I wrote this, I didn't really understand why I did the things that I did in relationships. I have learnt a lot through writing this all out, so now I want to share with you what I have learnt. I know I'm not the only woman in the world who has had these issues, or who will have them, or who is struggling to understand all her WTF moments. We may feel like we are alone but we're all going through the same thing, just in different ways. An incredible woman in my life recently told me one of her favourite quotes. I love the quote; it is 'We're all in the same storm, we're just in different boats.'

I've told you about the guys in my life, now let me continue pouring out my heart to you and see if I can finish piecing together the bits and pieces of the jigsaw puzzle I call my life.

As I wrote at the beginning of this story, I didn't think too highly of myself appearance-wise.

I know I'm a good person, I always try to do the right thing, I help people when I can, and I have always been like that. People who know me always say that I have a beautiful soul, they think I'm a good person, and people trust me and know I am going to do the right thing. I believe in the best in people, I always give more chances than people deserve. I'm the person who buys a homeless man a bag of groceries and gives them to him and not tells anyone I've done it; in the supermarket, if the person before me is counting their pennies and has to get items taken off their bill, I pay for them. I talk to strangers, I smile at everyone, and I help whenever I can with whatever I can. There are many good qualities to who I am, but they are also what brings me down.

I need to stop apologising for being me, I need to stop changing who I am and I need to learn to be unapologetically me.

Believe it or not, I have no regrets. Oh, don't get me wrong, I wish I had been better with money; I wish I had said no to some things, and I really don't like a lot of the crap I have been through. Please note: I am fully aware that others have been through far worse things than I could ever imagine. There are countries in our world that are at war, there are religions and cultures that strip women of their rights, and there are horrendous things happening.

But I have no regrets.

With Eddie, I learnt about romance and how amazing romance could be.

With George, I just knew things weren't right but I was too scared to accept that he was cheating on me, I began to look at sex as a way of keeping my partner happy.

But with George, I got my babies.

With Kent, I was abused. I was ashamed and I lived a life I had no idea how to get out of. But I did. I got out. I refuse to call myself a victim, I am a survivor. I learnt more about compassion, empathy, and being able to stand up for people. When I became a survivor, I became strong. I have become good at advocacy.

With Billy, I found a wild woman within. I learnt things about my body and about sex that I could never have imagined.

With Adam, I learnt about the powerful connection of falling in love with a person for their heart and soul and not the physical form. I also learnt how to recover from a truly broken heart.

With Oscar, I learnt to be careful with how I trusted people. I learnt that some people would fake feelings and relationships purely just to get a bit of a free ride in life.

With Luke, I learnt to be diplomatic in arguments. And believe it or not, I think I learnt more about myself—my strengths, weaknesses and faults—with Luke than I did with the others. Or perhaps when I was with Luke, I began to use all the lessons I had learnt.

All I know is now I am strong to the point of stubbornness. I have begun frustrating people around me by questioning their actions, by refusing to justify my own actions, or by saying no. I always do it gently and respectfully but people just aren't used to me doing that. In my personal life, things are definitely changing, and those close to me who love me and want the best for me are standing on the sidelines cheering me on.

Unfortunately, those who are close to me but are learning they can no longer control me are getting cranky with me and my 'disgusting attitude'. Yes, someone has told me my attitude is disgusting. There are moments when I do question if it is me, am I being selfish, self-centred and high maintenance? Then

I come to my senses; no, I am not being selfish. I am just no longer a pawn in their game.

Career-wise, I am soaring. Conducting myself with integrity and treating all people with respect. I am speaking up by sharing thoughts and opinions. By vocalising concerns with systems and policies, I have been given a few promotions over the last couple of years.

It has taken me a little while to complete this book, almost eighteen months in fact. Funnily enough, Luke and I seemed to have big arguments that resulted in him moving out every eighteen months. At the beginning of this book he had moved out, then he moved back in, and now we are at the end of the book, eighteen months later, and again he has left.

At times it has been a wonderful trip down memory lane; I've smiled and the more I wrote down the more I remembered. I've even found old photos of some of these guys in my life, and the one that got the biggest smile was Eddie. At other times, it has been quite confronting and difficult, with unwanted memories that I had buried deep in the darkest corners of my mind resurfacing. I won't lie, there have been times when I have shut the laptop and walked away from the computer for a while. Some of the resurfaced memories have been difficult to process.

Now I am 46 years old. I have been thinking that I have spent the last 30 years trying to keep others happy. Now I am older (though I don't feel old), I have less tolerance for bullshit, and I'm ready to enjoy my life.

My babies are adults and we enjoy doing things together. It's time for me to start doing the things I enjoy for myself that I haven't enjoyed as much as Luke didn't enjoy them; it's time to begin doing again the things I stopped or just didn't do as much.

When you are in a relationship with someone, you shouldn't have to change who you are, but together you change and grow. Together. Not separately. In the beginning, Luke and I were growing together. Then after a couple of breakups, we continued to grow, but we grew separately.

It's time for me to smile, laugh, live and love life. It's time for me to be me again.

I think after all I've been through, I am well and truly done with relationships. But then, who knows what will happen? Maybe Luke and I will be living together again in twelve months' time, all issues sorted and communication between us incredible. Maybe I will still be single. Maybe he will be with someone else (I have no idea how I will handle that if that happens).

After reading back on what I have written here, I am guessing that after a few months, I will start to feel lonely again. Who knows, perhaps I won't get lonely this time? One realisation I have had is I am lonelier with Luke at home, sitting on the lounge next to me and giving all his attention to his phone than I am when he is away and I'm on the lounge watching TV by myself. Maybe I won't get lonely this time. I guess I'll just have to wait and find out.

Chapter 21
The Relationship with Myself

What is this, you might ask? Well, it's not another chapter on going solo sexually. This chapter is about learning about myself. I'm trying to exhibit some emotional intelligence, and I have to tell you, it's very confronting. This whole experience of writing this book has been confronting.

I want the kind of romance where you know it's going to be amazing. I am a fiercely independent woman who wants to be treated like someone's queen. I get offended if people assume I can't do something, but feel special when someone does something for me.

I am a walking contradiction. God help any man who tries to figure me out; I can't even figure myself out. I wonder if Luke even had a chance.

I want the kind of kiss where you just know that it will be amazing. I want someone who will take the time to look into my eyes and slowly lean into the kiss. I want to know, as our lips move closer and you can feel the heated breath on your mouth, that the moment your lips touch, the rest of the world will disappear. I want the feeling that the entire universal existence is within that one kiss. I have had that with Luke but they only lasted a while. There is no reason for those types of kisses to stop.

And that doesn't always need to be a first kiss. That kind of kiss can happen anywhere, anytime. At the movies, at the beach, while stopped at traffic lights, on the dancefloor, while watching TV, while cooking dinner; anywhere, anytime. It's just romance. Plain and simple.

And as we have learnt throughout this story, in my adult life, I have chosen guys who only think romance is needed until the relationship turns solid and everyone is comfortable.

Those guys are wrong, so, so wrong. I am sure that the reason those relationships got to the point of both myself and the guy were feeling solid and comfortable with the relationship is due to the romance, affection, attention, thought and effort that both of us were putting into the relationship. The guys I have been with have just gotten lazy. I will admit that after a certain amount of time of trying to bring the romance back into the relationship, I didn't put in as much effort either.

I don't really want to give up on romance, I love romance. I love the way my heart beats just that little bit faster when think about cuddling into my man as we settle in for the evening. I love sending cheeky texts. I love putting notes in lunches or sharing random kisses. I enjoy cooking new meals that I think he would like. I think about ways to surprise and spoil him at birthdays at Christmas and sometimes for just no particular reason at all. I love it all, I miss it all. It hurts when you realise you don't have it anymore.

It hurts more being in the same house as that same man who used to make your heart skip a beat when you heard his car pull into the driveway and knowing that there were no more kisses and cuddles than it does for the relationship to be truly damaged. It hurts when he no longer wants to hear about your day and doesn't include you in plans. It's just painful.

Don't settle, dear readers, do not settle for something that you need to make up excuses for as to why it is good for you. End that. Be single. Grow. And then, when the time is right, I am positive that romance will find you again.

Well, that's what I keep telling myself anyway. Taking these actions is definitely easier to tell someone else to do than to do yourself. But I'm trying.

I'll allow myself to go through the process, I'll keep trying to bring back my shine. I'm sure there will be many times when I crumble and am desperate for one of Luke's amazing cuddles.

Who knows what will happen? Time will tell. Maybe there will be another book in a couple of years, perhaps it will be called 'Forty-Eight', and it will fill you in on all the happenings of the next couple of years.

Dear readers, thank you for reading my story. I hope you laughed a little at my romantic adventures. I hope I have helped you realise that you are not the only one who may have experienced odd moments in life. I hope you've found some comfort in my misery, as there are miseries we have all been through.

And I truly hope you all have a great network of friends around you who support and love you, and who are there for you without question, but always with a bottle of wine.

Love Always

X